OECD Public Governance Reviews

The Korean Public Procurement Service

INNOVATING FOR EFFECTIVENESS

Please cite this publication as:
OECD (2016), *The Korean Public Procurement Service: Innovating for Effectiveness*, OECD Public Governance Reviews, OECD Publishing, Paris.
http://dx.doi.org/10.1787/9789264249431-en

ISBN 978-92-64-24941-7 (print)
ISBN 978-92-64-24943-1 (PDF)

Series: OECD Public Governance Reviews
ISSN 2219-0406 (print)
ISSN 2219-0414 (online)

Photo credits: Cover © Kidsana Maimeetook/Shutterstock.com

Foreword

Public procurement represents a significant share of countries' economies, on average over 13% of GDP among OECD members. For many years, the OECD has assisted governments in reforming their public procurement systems through sharing international good practices, comparative data and conducting peer reviews at the national, sectorial and institutional level. Focus on public procurement has expanded from initial efforts on enhancing integrity to an overarching view of strategic public procurement as an essential mechanism for achieving government policy objectives, building citizen trust and fostering inclusive growth.

Central to this new direction in developing public procurement systems is an increased focus on efficiency through sound planning, design and delivery. Reducing administrative duplication for public officials and for private suppliers, transforming procurement practices through innovative digital governance tools and developing data to support policy decisions are all critical elements of advanced 21st century public procurement systems. As a G20 country with a well-developed procurement system, Korea's invitation to conduct this review demonstrates a commitment to continued improvement and innovation in public procurement reform.

This report on the Public Procurement Service (PPS) of Korea explores these issues through an assessment of the effectiveness and efficiency of PPS systems for e-procurement, framework agreements and support for social objectives. PPS has a wide range of responsibility over policy and purchasing in Korea, including responsibility for the Korean ON-line E-Procurement System (KONEPS), which processes nearly two-thirds of all public procurement in Korea – more than USD 60 billion annually. These responsibilities are executed in an integrated and strategic manner, driving continuous improvements for public procurement.

In each of the areas reviewed, Korea offers good practices that can inspire reform efforts in other countries. As a rare example of a truly comprehensive e-procurement system, KONEPS contributes substantially to efficiency and effectiveness of public procurement in Korea, saving an estimated USD 8 billion annually in administrative costs – mostly through reduced burden on suppliers – and allowing for payment in as little as four hours for many small and medium vendors.

Korean framework agreements serve as a model that achieves the benefits of centralised purchasing while remaining open to encourage competition, avoiding a common pitfall of such arrangements. In supporting social enterprises, Korea has adopted a holistic view that goes beyond merely directing contracts to targeted groups, supporting innovation and growth through the establishment of a variety of certification programmes. Liquidity for small and medium suppliers is also ensured through a variety of mechanisms.

Building on good practices identified by the OECD and experiences from other member countries, the peer review also highlights additional steps for improvement, including through a more centralised look at workforce training and development issues. Improving search functionalities and activating some features that are currently unused are among the recommendations for the e-procurement system, as well as the expanded collection and use of procurement data to drive policy decisions. Moving carefully to expand framework agreements into complex services and non-standard goods is recommended, along with appropriate training and skills development. A careful look at the variety and effectiveness of certification programmes, to determine whether simplification is possible, is also advised, together with the development of a central registry of social objective programmes to facilitate purchasing decisions.

In the context of evaluating such a mature and well-functioning public procurement system, these recommendations for improvements reflect the fact that public procurement involves a series of balanced approaches to complex policy decisions, and that continued development of innovative approaches can drive additional improvements to effectiveness. Korea offers a bright example of addressing many of these issues, one that can be pursued by others looking to achieve efficiency and value for money. It also demonstrates the value of a strategic approach to public procurement in driving broader government policy goals.

Through the implementation of a holistic, 21st century public procurement system, Korea embodies the OECD mission of designing, developing and delivering better policies for better lives.

Angel Gurría

OECD Secretary-General

Acknowledgements

The OECD expresses its gratitude to the Korean Public Procurement Service (PPS) for their welcoming support and open dialogue throughout the review process, in particular to Mr. Sangkyu Kim, Administrator of the Public Procurement Service, Mr. Sun-gu Ji, Director General of the International Goods Bureau, Ms. Kyung-Soon Chang, Head of Seoul Regional Public Procurement Service and Mr. Byeongcheol Im, Director of the International Cooperation Division. Special thanks are attributed to the staff of PPS, notably to Kang-il Seo, Kyungsuk Cho, and Minsook Hong for providing information, facilitating interviews and interpretation with relevant stakeholders and co-ordinating the peer review process.

As part of a series of peer reviews on public procurement in OECD, G20 and non-member economies, the review benefited from input provided by senior public procurement officials participating in the OECD Meeting of the Working Party of Leading Practitioners on Public Procurement held in Paris on 27-28 April 2015 and chaired by Lorna Prosper, Senior Director of Procurement Policy of the Office of the Comptroller General, Treasury Board of Canada Secretariat. Special thanks go to the lead reviewers: Andreas Nemec, Chief Executive Officer, Bundesbeschaffung GmbH, Austria and Karen Pica, Senior Management Analyst, Office of Federal Procurement Policy, Executive Office of the President of the United States.

Under the direction of Rolf Alter and János Bertók, this review was led by Paulo Magina and Jeremy McCrary. Valuable comments were received from Despina Pachnou, Emma Cantera, Matthieu Cahen and Minjoo Son. Editorial assistance was provided by Anastasia Slojneva, Julie Harris and Thibaut Gigou, and additional administrative assistance was provided by Anaisa Goncalves.

Table of contents

Tables

Figures

Abbreviations and acronyms

AoG	All-of-Government
BAI	Board of Audit and Inspection
BBG	*Bundesbeschaffung GmbH*
BRIAS	Bid Rigging Indicator Analysis System
CPB	Central Purchasing Body
EDI	Electronic Data Interchange
FSSI	Federal Strategic Sourcing Initiative
FTC	Fair Trade Commission
HUBZone	Historically Underutilized Business Zone
ICT	Information and Communications Technology
KONEPS	Korean ON-line E-Procurement System
KRW	Korean Won
MAS	Multiple Award Schedules
MOGAHA	Ministry of Government Administration and Home Affairs
NEP	New Excellent Product
PFL	Procurement Functional Leadership
PKI	Public Key Infrastructure
PPS	Public Procurement Service
PQ	Pre-Qualification
SMBA	Small and Medium Business Administration
SMEs	Small and Medium-sized Enterprises
SMSGC	Subcontract Management System for Government Contracts
UGAP	*Union des groupements d'achats publics*

Executive summary

Representing EUR 4.3 trillion per year in OECD countries, public procurement is a crucial pillar of strategic governance. As a substantial nexus between the public and private sphere as well as a critical channel for services delivery to citizens, public procurement conducted with integrity, transparency and accountability is essential to developing public trust. With governments facing continued budgetary pressures and demands to "do more with less," focus has increasingly turned to public procurement reform as a means of increasing efficiency and effectiveness for public services delivery.

In addressing these needs, countries are turning to e-procurement solutions and central purchasing bodies (CPBs). With application throughout the procurement cycle, information and communication technologies are replacing and transforming paper-based procurement practices. In addition to reducing costly administrative duplication, such tools increase efficiency to drive savings, and can yield greater transparency, accountability and access to public procurement opportunities. Similarly, CPBs can offer advantages in the form of savings through better bargaining power, the development of central sources of expertise and training, and the opportunity to truly understand markets in a way that goes beyond finding the lowest price to truly achieve better value for citizens.

In this context, the Korean Public Procurement Service (PPS) invited the OECD to assess the efficiency and function of its procurement system with a focus on the Korea ON-line E-Procurement System (KONEPS), Korean Multiple Award Schedule (MAS) framework agreements and support for social enterprises.

Key findings

KONEPS is an integrated e-procurement system which contributes substantially to the efficiency, effectiveness and integrity of public procurement in Korea. KONEPS addresses all phases of the procurement cycle, and transparency is provided through the publication of public procurement information. Access for stakeholders is assured through standardised and simplified processes, and through regular trainings and a help desk to answer questions about the system. This simple, ready access facilitates competition by lowering barriers to entry for suppliers and other public procurement stakeholders. Through the adoption of standardised forms and interconnection with other electronic systems, KONEPS generates administrative savings of approximately USD 8 billion per year, with more than 80% of these savings accruing to private sector participants.

Modular, flexible, scalable and secure development is also evident in KONEPS, through the addition of new functional modules in response to demands from stakeholders. Examples include new features such as KONEPS services for private-sector purchasers, and the implementation of a new virtual environment for enhanced security.

Implementation of MAS contracting offers good practices, particularly in the areas of standardisation, efficiency and competition. Offering MAS contracts on a rolling timetable encourages broad participation from suppliers, while standard processes for establishing and ordering from contracts lowers barriers for suppliers of all sizes by clarifying expectations.

Efficiency is driven through reduction of duplication, streamlining the function of the public procurement system. Since dedicated PPS contracting officials manage the work of establishing the MAS contracts, officials in other public-buying entities benefit by ordering with reduced burden and overlap, allowing them to focus their own efforts on purchases with high priority within their organisations. Competition is encouraged by providing an open-market environment for new vendors and by explicitly requiring second-stage competition in the case of large purchases.

PPS implementation of secondary policy objectives goes beyond the awarding of contracts to support liquidity and encourage growth among targeted social enterprises. While support for secondary policy objectives includes elements to set aside or otherwise provide a contract award advantage to social enterprises, a number of innovative approaches are also employed.

To support liquidity, small and medium-sized enterprises (SMEs) are entitled to an upfront payment of up to 70% of the value of a government contract. In many cases, SMEs are also entitled to instant payment upon presentation of an accepted invoice – and KONEPS integration facilitates this payment in as little as four working hours. A programme is in place to offer SMEs loans of up to 80% of the value of a government contract with no other collateral.

Additional programmes encourage growth and innovation through the awarding of certificates that allow for preferential purchasing or direct award. Awarded by both PPS and the Small and Medium Business Administration, these programmes include many specific certifications that provide distinct benefits. Excellent Government Supply Product certification, the highest offered, allows direct contracting with any public entity.

Key recommendations

In addition to these successes, the peer review also identified a number of recommendations that can be implemented to improve the efficiency and effectiveness of public procurement in Korea.

Across the areas of the review, additional efforts in support of professionalisation were identified. For the procurement workforce, these include co-ordinating training offerings and developing the procurement training certification. Development of a network of public buyers can support communication and knowledge management, as can the use of client management files to ensure smooth transitions. Integration of audit findings in the training curriculum can support incorporation of lessons learned.

Recommendations for improving the e-procurement function include developing or activating features such as improved search functionalities and an electronic auctions function. Data collection and use is being expanded, and this should continue in order to support the development of procurement indicators to monitor the efficiency of the public procurement system, providing a better evidence base for policy makers.

As a specific example, the availability of whole-of-government data can be used to support further expansion of MAS contracting, providing a better understanding of government demand. As the use of MAS expands to cover more services and non-standard goods, appropriate workforce training and skills requirements should be developed and implemented, including consideration of a commodity-management approach for complex services.

For social enterprises support, better metrics to evaluate the effectiveness and structure of certification programmes is recommended, as is the collection of a central listing of all mandatory and recommended requirements or goals. Better pacing of upgrades to KONEPS can lessen the training burden on small suppliers, and evaluating tenders from large suppliers on the basis of their support for SME subcontracts could provide an additional avenue for supporting small and medium-sized enterprises.

Chapter 1

Central purchasing in Korea: The Public Procurement Service

Established in 1949 as the Provisional Office of Foreign Supply, the Public Procurement Service (PPS) took on its current role as a central procurement agency of Korea in 1961. PPS has a variety of responsibilities related to the purchase and management of resources needed for public administration, all of which are undertaken with a focus on transparent and effective delivery of services while also contributing to savings through consolidation and centralisation as well as furthering economic development in Korea. The present chapter provides an introduction to public procurement in Korea generally, and a more detailed examination of the various roles undertaken by PPS. This includes presentations of the legal authorities that govern public procurement in Korea, the responsibilities and organisation of PPS, and detailed information regarding the scope of public procurement activities.

Public procurement in Korea

Legal authorities

The Act on Contracts to Which the State is a Party ("State Contract Act") establishes a principle under which the government engages in legal acts as a private economic entity. Under this system, special laws relevant to government contracts are applied with priority, as they provide exceptional provisions. Then the State Contract Act is applied. Finally, civil law principles relating to contracts, such as the Principle of Party Autonomy, Principle of Good Faith, and Principle of Abuse of Rights apply to matters not addressed in the special laws or State Contract Act.

As in many country contexts, the broad scope of public procurement requires the distribution of responsibilities among a number of relevant ministries. While the Ministry of Strategy and Finance in Korea has primary responsibility for central procurement (including housing PPS), the Ministry of Government Administration and Home Affairs; Land, Infrastructure and Transport; Trade, Industry and Energy; Health and Welfare; Employment and Labour; and the Small and Medium Business Administration all have legal authorities related to public procurement (see Table 1.1).

These acts are then supported in implementation through the development of more detailed enforcement decrees, enforcement ordinances and regulations. As an example, a list of established and announced regulations from the Ministry of Strategy and Finance that are relevant to public procurement is presented in Box 1.1.

Mandatory use of centralised processes

The public procurement system in Korea is comprised of a combination of centralised and decentralised procurement requirements, with legal requirements contained in different sources depending on the type of entity. Requirements for central government entities are contained in the State Contract Act; the Local Government Contract Act governs procurement by local government entities; and other public entities are governed by the Act on the Management of Public Institutions.

For central government agencies, the procurement of goods, services and construction works through PPS is mandatory when they exceed certain threshold amounts. This includes any construction projects valued at more than USD 2.54 million[1] (USD 254 300 for electric or communication projects), and commodity or services procurements with a value above USD 84 763. Central government entities are also required to purchase through PPS for goods or services with existing centralised contracts in place, whether they are unit price, third-party unit price or Multiple Award Schedule (MAS) framework contracts.

Over the last two decades, increased autonomy has been provided to local government entities to procure goods and services projects directly, through the reduction and elimination of mandatory thresholds for use of PPS (see Table 1.2). The requirements that local government entities, including educational institutions, use PPS for construction works projects have also been eliminated over time, as shown in Table 1.3.

Table 1.1. **Public procurement legal authorities in Korea**

Full title	Responsible authority	Description
Act on Contracts to Which the State is a Party (State Contract Act)	Ministry of Strategy and Finance	Prescribes basic rules on contracts made with central government organisations.
Act on Contracts to Which a Local Government is a Party (Local Government Contract Act)	Ministry of Government Administration and Home Affairs	Prescribes basic rules on contracts made with local autonomies.
Act on the Management of Public Institutions	Ministry of Strategy and Finance	Prescribes basic matters on management of public institutions.
Government Procurement Act	Ministry of Strategy and Finance (PPS)	Prescribes necessary matters related to operation and management of procurement business.
Framework Act on the Construction Industry	Ministry of Land, Infrastructure and Transport	Prescribes basic rules on survey, design, inspection, maintenance and technology management of construction works. Also stipulates necessary matters related to registering as a construction business, subcontracting of construction works and others.
Construction Technology Promotion Act	Ministry of Land, Infrastructure and Transport	Prescribes matters related to the advancement of construction technology and quality enhancement and safety management of construction works.
Electrical Construction Business Act	Ministry of Trade, Industry and Energy	Prescribes basic matters related to electrical construction business and technology management and subcontracting of electrical construction.
Small and Medium Enterprises Promotion Act (SMEs Promotion Act)	Small and Medium Business Administration	Prescribes matters related to strengthening the competitiveness of SMEs, business management and others.
Act on Facilitation of Purchase of Small and Medium Enterprise-Manufactured Products and Support for Development of Their Markets	Small and Medium Business Administration	Prescribes matters related to promotion of purchasing goods manufactured by SMEs, support for their market entry and others.
Framework Act on Small and Medium Enterprises	Small and Medium Business Administration	Prescribes basic matters related to policies to nurture SMEs, their visions and others.
Industrial Standardisation Act	Ministry of Trade, Industry and Energy	Prescribes matters related to dissemination of industrial standardisation and others.
Quality Control and Safety Management of Industrial Products Act	Ministry of Trade, Industry and Energy	Prescribes matters related to quality management and safety management of industrial products.
Government Organisation Act	Ministry of Government Administration and Home Affairs	Prescribes matters related to establishment, structure and scope of roles and functions of government organisation.
Framework Act on Low-Carbon Green Growth	Office for Government Policy Coordination (Prime Minister's Secretariat)	Prescribes matters related to creating an environment for low-carbon green growth and utilising green technology and industry as a growth engine.
Special Act on the Preferential Purchase of Products Manufactured by Persons with Severe Disabilities	Ministry of Health and Welfare	Prescribes matters related to support for preferential purchase of products manufactured by occupational rehabilitation centres and others which hire persons with severe disabilities.
Act on Support for Female-owned Businesses	Small and Medium Business Administration	Prescribes matters related to support for activities of female-owned businesses and their establishment.
Income Tax Act	Ministry of Strategy and Finance	Prescribes matters related to individual income and taxation.
Value-added Tax Act	Ministry of Strategy and Finance	Prescribes matters related to requirement and procedure of imposing value-added tax.
Social Enterprise Promotion Act	Ministry of Employment and Labour	Prescribes matters related to establishment, operation and promotion of social enterprises.

Source: PPS response to OECD internal questionnaire, 2014 with updates in 2015.

Box1.1. Regulations and public notice for government contracts

Regulations established by the Ministry of Strategy and Finance:

- general terms and conditions of construction contracts
- construction bid instruction
- general terms and conditions of commodity purchase contracts
- commodity purchase bid instruction
- general terms and conditions of technical service
- technical service bid instruction
- qualification screening criteria
- guidance to pre-qualification screening
- government bid/contract execution criteria
- estimated price preparation criteria
- guidance to joint subcontract administration
- negotiated contract signing criteria
- guidance to comprehensive contract signing
- arbitration on international contract dispute mediation committee
- bid price standards for lowest-price system
- criteria for the successful bidder through a batch bidding.

Regulations announced by the Ministry of Strategy and Finance:

- announced price decided by the Minister of Strategy and Finance for the Act on Government Contracts
- projects announced by the Minister of Strategy and Finance.

Source: Korean Ministry of Strategy and Finance

Table 1.2. **Threshold amount for goods and services purchasing by local government entities**[1]

	Prior to 2004	Prior to 2006	Prior to 2008	Current
Must use PPS	Above USD 42 381 (USD 50 000 for foreign procurement)	Above USD 59 334 (USD 100 000 for foreign procurement)	Above USD 84 763 (USD 200 000 for foreign procurement)	Fully autonomous
May buy autonomously	Less than USD 42 381 (USD 50 000 for foreign procurement)	Less than USD 59 334 (USD 100 000 for foreign procurement)	Less than USD 84 763 (USD 200 000 for foreign procurement)	

1. The values for foreign procurement in this table were originally presented in USD.

Source: PPS response to OECD internal questionnaire, 2014 with updates in 2015.

Table 1.3. **Threshold amount for construction works by local government entities**

	Prior to 2005	Prior to 2007	Prior to 2008	Prior to 2010	Current
Must use PPS	Pre-qualification (PQ) construction, alternative tender construction, turnkey	PQ construction over USD 17 million, alternative tender construction, turnkey	PQ construction over USD 42.4 million, alternative tender construction, turn key	Alternative tender construction, turn key	Fully autonomous
May buy autonomously	Others	Others included in PQ construction less than USD 17 million	Others included in PQ construction less than USD 42.4 million	Others included in all PQ construction	

Source: PPS response to OECD internal questionnaire, 2014 with updates in 2015.

However, many still choose to request purchasing through PPS as a matter of policy, to take advantage of the centralised expertise that PPS offers. Local government entities are also still required to purchase goods and services through established PPS contracts in the case of unit price, third-party unit price, or MAS framework contracts.

Other public entities and quasi-government agencies are required to purchase through PPS for "competitive goods," as defined in the SMEs Promotion Act, above certain thresholds announced by the Minister of Strategy and Finance. This requirement applies when purchasing competitive goods manufactured by SMEs either under open competition, or in the case of unit price, third-party unit price, or MAS framework contracts.

Despite the increased autonomy allowed to local government entities and other public entities, the number of PPS user entities has increased by almost 10% since 2010, with only 0.5% of this increase coming from new central government entities (see Table 1.4).

Table 1.4. **Number of public entities registered with PPS as "user entities"**

	Total	Central govt. entities	Local govt. entities			Other entities			
			Local govts.	Boards of education	Public enterprises	Quasi-governmental entities	Other public entities	Local govt. owned enterprises	Misc.
2010	42 405	5 145	6 713	10 837	864	1 020	445	163	17 218
2011	43 708	5 195	6 772	10 994	945	1 088	403	175	18 136
2012	45 055	5 245	6 836	11 121	966	1 100	425	186	19 176
2013	46 773	5 349	6 895	11 234	992	1 127	430	197	20 549
2014	48 681	5 430	6 944	11 368	1 005	1 333	461	206	22 934

Source: PPS response to OECD internal questionnaire, 2014 with updates in 2015.

These users include other entities that are entrusted to carry out tasks on behalf of, or act as agents of, central government or local government entities pursuant to relevant laws or regulations, which are approved by PPS on an individual basis. Registration for such external entities requires appropriate documentation, such as a certified copy of business registration for private schools, certificates of incorporation and articles of association for social welfare entities, or a copy of the entrustment contract, for other entities entrusted to carry out business on behalf of government.

Size of public procurement

Statistics on overall public procurement in Korea are reported annually by the Small and Medium Business Administration (SMBA). SMBA carries out this data collection and reporting as part of its legal mandate to report on the progress achieved in using public procurement to support social objectives, such as the promotion of small and medium-sized enterprises.

Data for total public procurement volume includes the procurement of goods, services and public works by 516 entities that include central government, local government entities, boards of education, public enterprises, quasi-governmental entities, state-subsidised entities, local-government owned enterprises and public entities established by special laws. Procurement by the military of personal consumables, commercial goods and services is included, but other elements of defence procurement (for example, the development and purchase of weaponry) are not included. Procurement by the legislative and judicial branches is also excluded.

Total procurement volume peaked in 2009 as a result of stimulus spending measures in response to the economic crisis, and then declined as this spending decreased during 2010 and 2011. Since then, total procurement volume has again been rising incrementally, as demonstrated in Figure 1.1.

Figure 1.1. **Total procurement volume in Korea**

In USD billions

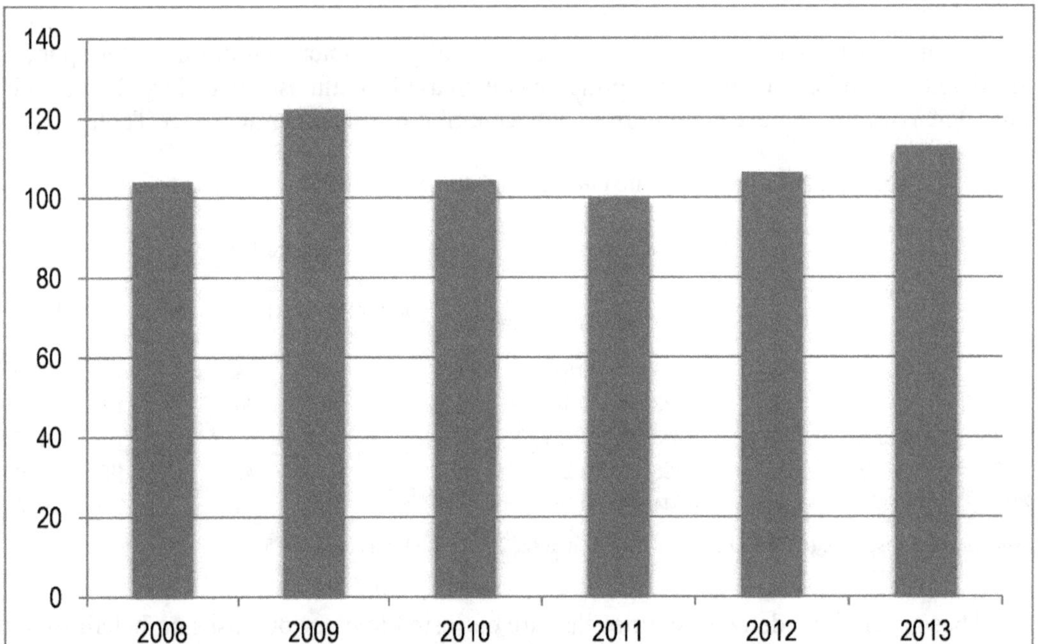

Source: PPS response to OECD internal questionnaire, 2014 with updates in 2015.

PPS functions

Overview

The mission of PPS is "to provide the best value service to its clients, save national budget spending and contribute to economic development by procuring and managing resources for public administration." This mission is carried out through a variety of independent and interrelated functions (see Box 1.2). As with calculations for overall procurement volume, procurement of design or purchase of weapons systems and other defence procurement is excluded, but the purchase of some commodities and services in support of soldiers is included.

Box 1.2. **PPS functions**

- Procurement of goods and services
  - Domestic procurement: Goods, services and leases produced or supplied domestically
  - Foreign procurement: Goods and services produced or supplied from overseas in accordance with international standard practices
- Construction works and services
- Operation and management of the Korea ON-line E-Procurement System (KONEPS)
- Operation of stockpiling business
  - Stockpiles and releases major raw materials including aluminium to ensure price stability and to support SMEs
- Management of government goods and property
  - Establish policies to manage government-owned goods and supervision
  - Inspection of the management of government property

To support these functions, PPS also undertakes a number of procurement business processes. For goods and services, and the stockpiling function, this includes logistics management and supply processes. For construction works, PPS offers a broad range of business services throughout the process, including total project cost review, tailored development, and project management services following contract award. Additionally, other business projects, related or allowed by relevant law, are undertaken as appropriate.

To support this work, PPS is divided into a number of central divisions, bureaus and offices, as well as 11 regional offices and 2 overseas offices (see Figure 1.2). The total staff is 970, with 442 (45.5%) located at headquarters.

Figure 1.2. **PPS organisational chart**

Source: Korean Public Procurement Service, www.pps.go.kr/eng/jsp/about/organization.eng (accessed 16 October 2015).

PPS roles and functions are wider than other central purchasing bodies (CPBs) in OECD. Almost all OECD member countries having a CPB (90%) have a CPB at the central level; while more than half (52%) also have distinct CPBs at the regional level. Additionally, in some OECD member countries CPBs are state-owned enterprises (15%), as in Finland, France and Italy. The majority of CPBs in OECD member countries (81%) either operate under a line ministry or function as a government agency.

In most OECD member countries, CPBs undertake the role of acting as a contracting authority aggregating demand and purchasing (85%), and as manager of the system for awarding framework agreements or other consolidated instruments, from which contracting authorities then order (73%). In contrast, in a few OECD member countries CPBs co-ordinate training for public officials in charge of public procurement (38%) and establish policies for contracting authorities (31%). CPBs in Greece, Ireland, Switzerland, the United Kingdom and the United States exercise all the above-mentioned functions whereas CPBs in nine OECD member countries (35%) have a single role, e.g. in Estonia, Luxembourg, and Poland (see Table 1.5).

Table 1.5. **The role of the central purchasing body in selected OECD member countries and non-member economies**

	CPBs act as a contracting authority aggregating demand and purchasing	CPBs act as manager of the national system awarding framework agreements or other consolidated instruments, from which contracting authorities then order	CPBs co-ordinate training for public officials in charge of public procurement	CPBs establish policies for contracting authorities
Australia	•			
Austria	•	•		
Belgium		•		
Canada	•	•	•	
Chile		•	•	•
Denmark		•		•
Estonia		•		
Finland	•			
France	•	•	•	
Germany	•			
Greece	•	•	•	•
Hungary	•	•		
Ireland	•	•	•	•
Italy	•	•		
Korea	•	•	•	
Luxembourg	•			
New Zealand	•	•	•	
Norway	•			
Poland	•			
Portugal	•	•		
Slovak Republic	•			
Slovenia	•	•		
Spain	•	•		•
Switzerland	•	•	•	•
United Kingdom	•	•	•	•
United States	•	•	•	•
Brazil	•		•	•
Colombia		•	•	•
OECD26	22	19	10	8

Source: OECD (2015a), *Government at a Glance 2015*, OECD Publishing, Paris, http://dx.doi.org/10.1787/gov_glance-2015-en.

PPS also supports its work through the operation of a special budget account, which provides a number of advantages. Revenue in the fund is primarily generated through the fees charged by PPS for contracts made on behalf of public organisations (see Box 1.3). The special account is used to support PPS labour costs and other contract-related expenses. In addition, the special account supports a revolving fund that is used to expedite payment to suppliers on behalf of the buying entity or end user, whose payment is then eventually returned to the special account. This process has reduced payment time to as little as four hours following approved delivery and inspection, in some cases. This function only applies to domestic procurement of goods and services, construction works and foreign procurement contracts are always paid directly from the buying entity or end user. Finally, the special account is also used to support stable supply and support for SMEs through the stockpiling function.

Box 1.3. **Fees for PPS services**

The fees charged by PPS vary, depending on several factors. Both the nature of the procurement and the role that PPS plays in the process are the primary factors. Procurement fees were last updated in November 2014 by Article 10 of the Enforcement Decree of the Government Procurement Act. The following is a general description of the fees applied to different categories, while more detailed calculation methodology and rates are introduced on the PPS website.

Purchase in local currency (KRW): Fees are applied at a diminishing rate according to the amount of the contract. For contracts below USD 17 000, the fee is fixed at USD 178. For contracts between USD 17 000 and USD 42 400, the fee is fixed at USD 450. For the amount exceeding USD 42 400, USD 84 800, USD 848 000 and USD 8.48 million, rates of 1.07%, 0.76%, 0.48% and 0.38% apply respectively.

For orders through existing contracts, including unit price, third-party unit price or MAS framework contracts, a flat rate of 0.54% applies regardless of the amount of the contract (however, for oil products, a 0.27% rate applies).

Purchase in foreign currency: The fees are applied at a diminishing rate similar to those for purchase in local currency according to the amount of the contract. More specifically, 1.2% of the amount is charged as a fee for contracts below USD 1 million and for the amounts exceeding USD 1 million, USD 5 million and USD 10 million, rates of 0.9%, 0.7% and 0.4% apply respectively.[1]

Construction work contracts: Similarly for purchasing, fees are applied at a diminishing rate but they differ as well according to procurement process. The highest fees are charged for lowest-price selection, then pre-qualification (PQ), non-PQ, alternative and turnkey contracts. Different rates also apply between central government and bodies' contracts as well as those from local purchasing entities: fees are lower for local entities' contracts overall. Further, construction work above USD 8.48 million by local entities is exempt from fees if it is funded by a government subsidy.

Purchase of technology/service: Fees are higher for purchase of services compared to others. They are applied as well at a diminishing rate and differ slightly for services such as planning and construction supervision and management services.

Tailored service: Fees vary for review service, management of planning and design and construction management. Fees are applied based on the budget for the construction work, and vary according to the degree of the PPS's involvement. The rate at which the fee is charged decreases as the construction budgets based on which the fee is calculated increases.

Review of total work expenses: For review of total work expenses, PPS charges relatively low fees. More specifically, for review of appropriateness of design, fees are charged based on the amount of the work requested to be reviewed and, for amounts below USD 8.48 million, the rate of 0.04% fee is charged for central government bodies and local entities. However for amounts exceeding USD 8.48 million, local entities benefit from lower fees of 0.02% whereas central government bodies are charged the same rate of 0.04%. Furthermore, for reviews of price fluctuation, the same rate of 0.1% is charged for both central and local government bodies. In cases where PPS is carrying out the construction work contract, this fee is waived.

1. The values in the "Purchase in foreign currency" paragraph were originally presented in USD.

Source: PPS response to OECD internal questionnaire, 2014 with updates in 2015.

PPS procurement statistics

Procurement of goods, services and construction works contracting through PPS represents approximately one-third of public procurement spending in Korea (see Table 1.6).

Table 1.6. **PPS procurement as percentage of total procurement volume**

In USD billions

	2009	2010	2011	2012	2013
Total procurement volume	103.7	88.5	84.6	90.2	95.8
PPS procurement	36.2	32.0	28.2	29.0	32.1
Percentage	34.9%	36.2%	33.3%	32.2%	33.5%

Source: PPS response to OECD internal questionnaire, 2014 with updates in 2015.

A more detailed breakdown of PPS procurement, including foreign procurement, is provided in Table 1.7. In addition to the construction procurement conducted by PPS, construction-related services including construction project management, cost review, and total project cost review are provided for projects with values reflected in Table 1.8. Details related to the PPS commodity stockpiling function are provided in Table 1.9.

Table 1.7. **Annual procurement by PPS**

In USD billions

		2009	2010	2011	2012	2013	2014
Procurement contracting total		37.4	32.5	28.8	29.4	32.5	28.8
Domestic procurement	Goods (includes leases)	13.5	12.3	12.8	15.9	14.3	15.9
	Services	2.5	2.4	2.4	3.1	2.6	3.2
	Subtotal	16.0	14.7	15.2	19.0	16.9	19.1
Foreign procurement		1.2	0.5	0.6	0.4	0.4	0.4
Construction procurement	Construction	20.3	17.0	12.7	12.8	11.9	9.0
	Related services	Included in "domestic" category	0.3	0.3	0.3	0.3	0.3
	Subtotal	20.3	17.3	13.0	13.1	12.2	9.2

Source: PPS response to OECD internal questionnaire, 2014 with updates in 2015.

Table 1.8. **Value of projects for which PPS provides construction-related services**

In USD billions

	2009	2010	2011	2012	2013	2014
Construction project management	2.4	2.8	2.0	2.6	2.3	1.0
Total project cost review	16.1	7.7	8.6	6.2	7.0	9.8
Cost review	1.9	1.3	0.7	0.9	2.0	1.7
Total	20.4	11.8	11.4	9.7	11.2	12.6

Source: PPS response to OECD internal questionnaire, 2014 with updates in 2015.

Table 1.9. **PPS commodity stockpiling operation**

In USD millions

		2009	2010	2011	2012	2013
Commodity stockpiling	Purchase	581.8	274.3	307.5	477.0	539.0
	Release	357.4	315.5	558.8	362.6	401.2

Source: Public Procurement Service (2013), "2013 annual report: Public Procurement Service, the Republic of Korea", www.pps.go.kr/eng.

Public procurement training and knowledge management

Considering the economic importance of public procurement, it is essential that procurement professionals have adequate knowledge and skills necessary to manage the interface with the private sector and mitigate the potential for corruption. As public procurement systems are used more frequently to pursue additional policy objectives, there is increased complexity involved in balancing these objectives, and a procurement workforce with the capacity to address these challenges is necessary. OECD work in public procurement has demonstrated that this is an area where many countries face challenges. In fact, adequate capability and management of the procurement function was identified as an area for improvement by 48.4% of respondents during the monitoring of the 2008 OECD "Recommendation of the Council on Enhancing Integrity in Public Procurement". In more than one-third of OECD countries, procurement is not recognised as a specific profession. This focus on procurement workforce capacity is recognised in the 2015 OECD "Recommendation of the Council on Public Procurement" (hereafter, the "OECD Recommendation"). See Box 1.4 for the section on professionalisation in the OECD Recommendation.

Box 1.4. **OECD Recommendation on professionalisation**

IX. RECOMMENDS that Adherents develop a procurement workforce with the **capacity** to continually deliver value for money efficiently and effectively.

To this end, Adherents should:

Ensure that procurement officials meet high professional standards for knowledge, practical implementation and integrity by providing a dedicated and regularly updated set of tools, for example, sufficient staff in terms of numbers and skills, recognition of public procurement as a specific profession, certification and regular trainings, integrity standards for public procurement officials and the existence of a unit or team analysing public procurement information and monitoring the performance of the public procurement system.

Provide attractive, competitive and merit-based career options for procurement officials, through the provision of clear means of advancement, protection from political interference in the procurement process and the promotion of national and international good practices in career development to enhance the performance of the procurement workforce.

Promote collaborative approaches with knowledge centres such as universities, think tanks or policy centres to improve skills and competences of the procurement workforce. The expertise and pedagogical experience of knowledge centres should be enlisted as a valuable means of expanding procurement knowledge and upholding a two-way channel between theory and practice, capable of boosting application of innovation to public procurement systems.

Source: OECD (2015b), "Recommendation of the Council on Public Procurement", www.oecd.org/corruption/recommendation-on-public-procurement.htm.

Training for procurement officials and for private sector stakeholders is provided through a number of sources in Korea. Centrally, PPS operates a training facility that provides training for approximately 5 000 people annually. This training centre offers residential courses of two or three days for PPS employees, employees of other central, local and public entities, and for private sector participants. For suppliers, PPS training usually consists of a two-day course covering public tenders generally and the use of the KONEPS system. Costs for buying entities are around USD 120 for a three-day course (including room and board at the training centre dormitory), while costs for a two-day course for suppliers are approximately USD 82.[2] The PPS training facility is also responsible for the certification process for procurement officials. In addition to the central training facility, 9 of the 11 regional PPS offices also offer training courses for KONEPS users.

Training is also available from a variety of other sources. The Federation of Small and Medium Enterprises, which is not a governmental entity, but a legal entity in the public interest, established by Small and Medium Enterprise Cooperatives Act, offers training for its members. This training programme is a one-day, comprehensive course in how to participate in public tenders and how to use KONEPS. It is offered region by region, and each region is served by one or two courses annually. Other trade associations, such as the Construction Association of Korea, also provide training relevant for their members. Private sector training offerings on the use of KONEPS are also widely available, with third-party training providers basing their curricula on KONEPS manuals published by PPS.

Recommendations on training and knowledge management

Despite these training availabilities, Korea faces some challenges in the area of procurement workforce development. At a general level, the lack of co-ordination among training offerings yields potential for duplication of effort. Though PPS cannot control or manage the training offerings conducted by third parties, a better understanding of those offerings, and a better integration of the curriculum of the PPS training centre based on that understanding, could potentially lead to better targeting of training resources. Additional attention to the procurement certificate programme is also warranted. Though the certificate is offered and managed by the PPS training centre, there was no clear indication that achieving certification yielded any particular benefits for a public procurement official. Capturing these training offerings for online sharing or otherwise developing online training materials or courses could also expand the number of users who can benefit from these efforts, as well as provide an always-available resource for refreshing knowledge as needed.

As an integrity measure, to ensure that public officials do not develop long-term attachments to particular contacts, the Korean civil service includes a requirement that individuals rotate through different positions every two or three years. This is a practice that is also followed in other civil service systems (see the German example in Box 1.5), but it can pose some challenges in the context of public procurement officials. For an organisation like PPS, it offers a clear benefit, as individuals who transfer through different divisions receive a broad experience with a number of different public procurement issues, through the course of a career. For other central government entities, where procurement is simply one function (usually located in the General Service Division) among many, it means that individuals responsible for public procurement are only engaged in that activity for a relatively short period of time. In such circumstances, defining an attractive career path related to public procurement can be a challenge.

Box 1.5. **Staff rotation in the German civil service**

The basis for the civil service rotation practice in Germany can be found in No. 4.2 of the Federal Government Directive concerning the Prevention of Corruption in the Federal Administration, which reads:

"*The length of staff assignments in areas especially vulnerable to corruption shall in principle be limited; as a rule, it should not exceed a period of five years. If an assignment must be extended beyond this period, the reasons shall be recorded for the file.*"

The (formal) determination of *areas especially vulnerable to corruption* in that given sense has to regularly take place according to No. 2 of that directive, and is conducted according to a risk assessment system in place on the federal level (the states - *Länder* - maintain their own systems). According to the Directive concerning the Prevention of Corruption, and as further explained in the recommendations for its application (No. 3 in the brochure "Rules on Integrity"), each agency has to assess the areas of activity within the agency which are especially vulnerable to corruption, and to apply certain measures for staff entrusted with them. The rotation principle is one of them.

According to the Recommendation on Preventing Corruption, in areas of activity especially vulnerable to corruption,

- after identifying special vulnerability to corruption for the first time,
- after organisational or procedural changes,
- after changes to assigned tasks, or
- after no more than five years,
- the need for conducting a risk analysis should be examined.

This analysis involves a brief examination of the effectiveness of existing safeguards for each area of activity especially vulnerable to corruption; if the brief examination points to a need for action, a risk analysis is to be conducted. If action is needed, then the organisation and processes and/or personnel assignments are examined to see how they can be changed. In this case, the risk analysis will include recommendations and/or order additional measures.

In the case of exceptions authorised by the Federal Government Directive, the most typical reasons why members of staff posted in areas especially vulnerable to corruption had been remaining on the same post for more than five years are (in that order):

- specialists who cannot rotate
- other members of staff with specific knowledge which cannot be replaced, having due regard to continuity,
- members of staff who will very soon leave active service,
- members of staff who will soon change over to another position,
- members of staff for whom an appropriate other position on the same remuneration level cannot be provided.

In such cases, the Recommendation on Preventing Corruption in the Federal Administration indicates:

"*[i]f in exceptional cases rotation is not possible due to the nature of operations or to (personnel) management considerations (e.g. lack of expert staff), then other appropriate and effective measures to prevent corruption should be used instead (e.g. extending the application of the principle of greater scrutiny, working in teams and exchanging tasks within organisational units, transferring responsibilities, intensifying administrative and task-related supervision).*"

Box 1.5. **Staff rotation in the German civil service** *(continued)*

Such *other appropriate and effective measures to prevent corruption* can include the application of the "principle of greater scrutiny" (co-signature requiring a second staff member to check work results) or intensifying administrative and task-related supervision.

In Germany, most corruption cases in the past had been committed by members of staff who were on the same post for more than five years. As "situational corruption" is very rare in Germany, and corruption cases rather concern "structural corruption", third parties first have to "invest" in the relationship with the member of staff who is to be corrupted. Such "investment" does not pay once it is clear that the relevant member of staff will be rotating to another position in some years. If third parties try to build up good relations with administrative staff, the purpose is rather not to gain sympathy from a specific member of staff, but rather to maintain a good working relationship with the agency as such.

The purpose of the introduction of the rotation principle is not only to prevent corruption. Many agencies, in particular ministries, it also allows to regularly allow a person who is new to a position to have a "fresh view" on the matters that he or she is now responsible for. It is encouraged that, in particular on specific higher positions, members of staff are generalists who gain experience in many fields of work, and who are used to getting acquainted with new tasks quickly. The experience gained in former positions allows them to identify crosslinks between specific subjects. For this reason, according to many staff development plans, promotion to a higher position (and remuneration level) requires a specified number of different positions held on the former level; in many cases, this forms a mandatory prerequisite for such promotion.

Source: Adapted from Federal Ministry of the Interior (2014), "Rules on integrity", www.bmi.bund.de/SharedDocs/Downloads/EN/Broschueren/2014/rules-on-integrity.html.

For this reason, the development of methods and procedures for knowledge management becomes very important. One example, disclosed during the fact-finding mission, was the development of a survey report by a procurement official designed to identify all of the various secondary policy requirements that applied to public procurement. In addition to secondary policy objectives that apply to all of the government, some ministries and offices have additional requirements or recommendations to pursue social policy objectives through public procurement. In this case, the official's report identified 8-10 mandatory requirements, and up to 46 recommended procurement priorities. While this report was developed independently to help procurement officials manage internal prioritisation at a central government agency, central identification of all of the objectives required by law and regulation, presented in a simplified format, would be a useful tool, and a well-designed online presentation of such a tool could also allow individual ministries or entities to append their own specific requirements for easier reference.

The fact-finding mission also identified that there was no formal technical mechanism through which information could be shared more broadly among the public procurement workforce. Some opportunities for knowledge sharing occur - for example, regional procurement consultation meetings held each year bring together public procurement officials from various central government agencies – but they are one-off, ad hoc opportunities. One means of addressing this circumstance would be the development and support of a network of public buyers as an ongoing, regular forum for communication among public procurement officials in Korea. While regular in-person meetings might prove cost prohibitive, a dedicated and central online forum that could allow both communication and the collection and sharing of relevant information could provide a better sense of community and serve as a substantial support mechanism for new public buyers, and a valuable source of information over time.

While the buying entities and suppliers interviewed during the fact-finding mission were generally very satisfied with the level of support they received from PPS, both in terms of the call centre and the availability of staff to support their activities, one buyer mentioned an additional challenge that results from the rotation policy for civil servants: occasionally as one staff member rotates out and a new one rotates in, there are some delays in connecting with the new staff member responsible for the account. Better management of client relationships, for example through the creation of a detailed client file and a protocol for making contact when responsibilities are transferred, could address this issue.

Oversight of the public procurement function

Proper internal and external controls are an important element of a well-functioning public procurement system, and the OECD Recommendation contains additional details regarding necessary considerations (see Box 1.6). Public procurement activities in Korea are subjected to oversight both internally, in the form of an audit office for each central agency, as well as externally through the activities of the Board of Audit and Inspection of Korea (BAI) and the Fair Trade Commission (FTC).

Box 1.6. **OECD Recommendation on accountability**

XII. RECOMMENDS that Adherents apply oversight and control mechanisms to support **accountability** throughout the public procurement cycle, including appropriate complaint and sanctions processes.

To this end, Adherents should:

…

Ensure that internal controls (including financial controls, internal audit and management controls), and external controls and audits are co-ordinated, sufficiently resourced and integrated to ensure:

- the monitoring of the performance of the public procurement system;
- the reliable reporting and compliance with laws and regulations as well as clear channels for reporting credible suspicions of breaches of those laws and regulations to the competent authorities, without fear of reprisals;
- the consistent application of procurement laws, regulations and policies;
- a reduction of duplication and adequate oversight in accordance with national choices; and
- independent ex-post assessment and, where appropriate, reporting to relevant oversight bodies.

Source: OECD (2015b), "Recommendation of the Council on Public Procurement", www.oecd.org/corruption/recommendation-on-public-procurement.htm.

Audit authorities

PPS has in place both *ex ante* and *ex post* audit processes. The PPS Audit Team supervises execution and contract process of contracts (above certain price thresholds) executed under the budget of PPS or procured by PPS where certain risks are expected. Details regarding the PPS audit activities are contained in Table 1.10.

Table 1.10. **Scope of PPS audit activities**

Types of audit	Area of audit	Information audited
Ongoing audit	E-procurement system	Bid-rigging and price collusions Appropriateness and legality of electronic bidding execution Appropriateness of change in qualification criteria including notified qualification conditions, starting date of bidding, and reserve price Other general management issues of e-procurement system
Ex ante audit	Enforcement of main policies	Enforcement of policies or projects that are categorised as main policies or main projects that require progress assessment or review of the results
	Contracts for goods and services	The choice of awarding method of contracts of total amount estimated to be above USD 2 500
	Budget management	Execution of more than USD 8 500 per one of the following budget classes: • Utility + overhead costs • Maintenance cost of facility equipment • Equipment costs • Extra costs on equipment • Property acquisition costs • Budget account that is executed, executed for other purposes, carried forward or settled • The decision on choice or change of the organisation's main bank of transaction • Official meeting where more than 100 people participate (e.g. workshop)
	Goods management	Stock management change of more than USD 42 400 of book amount Sale or disposal of stock of more than USD 42 400 of book amount Loss and damage disposal
	Other	Items prescribed by the Head of the PPS to be audited *ex ante* Main terms of human resources management including appointment of an employee, rewards and disciplinary actions Management of affiliated organisations
Inspection audit	Inspection of goods	Inspection of goods (on items selected during *ex ante* audit)

Source: PPS response to OECD internal questionnaire, 2014 with updates in 2015.

For completed contracts, there are two types of *ex post* audits conducted by the PPS Audit and Inspection Officer. A number of regular audits occur each year; contracts are usually selected using information available in the KONEPS data warehouse, and the PPS Audit and Inspection Officer then inspects them for compliance. Additionally, targeted or themed audits are possible on an ad hoc basis. These audits usually occur in response to challenges from suppliers with respect to a particular contract action. They may also include a focus on a particular subject, for example the operation of the system or a particular feature of its use. PPS does not currently track the number or percentage of contracts subjected to more detailed audit, as part of either the regular or ad hoc process, but estimates that approximately 10% of all contract actions are reviewed in more detail by the internal PPS Audit and Inspection Officer. Detailed audit requires substantial time and resources. To most effectively utilise limited resources, PPS focuses on developing analytical techniques that utilise information from the KONEPS data warehouse in order to identify problems in general procurement processes.

PPS has responsibility for contracts established by PPS. Other contracts issued through KONEPS by other buying entities are subjected to oversight from their own internal audit offices. Additionally, the BAI has authority to review public procurement activity. The Board of Audit and Inspection Act gives the BAI broad access to data from central government agencies. PPS does not maintain a specific data-sharing agreement or direct data link with the BAI or with audit offices in other organisations, but the information available in the KONEPS data warehouse is generally sufficient to support these needs. As the KONEPS data warehouse contains more information than is publicly available, the BAI or other audit office will ask the PPS Audit and Inspection Officer for the data. In cases where the audit office requests data in a new form or format, the PPS IT division is capable of responding quickly to address the need.

These audits are generally focused on contract matters and compliance, focusing on contracts themselves, though some audits focus on the overall results of the procurement system. If illicit conduct is found during the course of an audit, the relevant procurement officer is penalised, depending on the severity of the problem. In minor cases, a warning may be issued, but in more serious cases penalties can include suspension of employment, deduction of wages, demotion or termination. With respect to the contract action, the application of civil law indicates that the only case where a contract is terminated is when the basis of the contract was legally void, for example in cases of deception. In other cases, the signed contract is still considered valid, despite any problems identified by an audit. In these cases, dissatisfied suppliers may bring legal action, but a successful suit would result in payment for damage rather than the dissolution of the contract.

Recommendations on audit and oversight

There is no formal and ongoing collaboration with the PPS Public Procurement Training Institute to capture the audit results as inputs into training development. Instead, most errors identified through audits are disseminated on an ad hoc basis, for instance through an audit fact sheet or through meetings of the headquarters and regional offices. PPS also looks for situations where a problematic audit finding could be addressed through a modification of KONEPS; in such cases the Audit and Inspection Officer will request that the information technology (IT) division update the system to address the potential problem. While these steps are important, finding a means of more fully integrating the results of audit activities into the training of procurement officers could yield benefits for the system.

Fair Trade Commission

The Fair Trade Commission (FTC) works with public buying entities to identify cartel activity and potential cases of bid rigging in public procurement. This work is particularly relevant at this time, as a number of potential cases related to increased spending in response to the 2009 economic crisis have been identified. During 2009 and 2010, Korea launched a number of large public works projects in a short period of time, and there are now claims that contractors colluded to divide this work.

To identify cases of collusion, the FTC traditionally relied on voluntary reporting by cartel members seeking leniency, and on reports by competing suppliers. These remain the most reliable sources of identification of potential collusion. In 2006, the FTC developed the Bid Rigging Indicator Analysis System (BRIAS) to supplement these methods of identification.

Drawing information directly from KONEPS, BRIAS looks to data elements including bidding price (as a ratio compared to reference price), the number of participants, and the competition method, and applies a formula that generates a potential bid-rigging score. If above a certain threshold, this then suggests the need to collect more information regarding the contract action. Based on this closer look, an investigation is opened in cases where it is warranted.

BRIAS collects information from KONEPS on a daily basis, and each month the system is run on collected data from the previous month. For goods and services, BRIAS is run on tenders above USD 423 800. For public works, the threshold is USD 4.2 million. As of 2012, BRIAS was run on 20 000-30 000 biddings per year; of approximately 20 000 runs in 2012, the system generated 200 hits that warranted an additional look. The establishment of this kind of automated system for the detection of red flags in public procurement is a good practice implemented successfully in other countries such as Brazil (see Box 1.7).

Whether identified through BRIAS or through traditional means, investigation of potential cases of collusion involves collection of additional information from PPS followed by site visitations and other investigative steps to find evidence of information exchange. These investigations can take anywhere from one to three years, from initial reporting to final verdict, and the FTC has established a separate investigation unit focused solely on public procurement. When found guilty, sanctions can range from orders for corrective action, which are essentially warnings for minor offenses, through a financial penalty of up to 10% of the contract volume involved. Additional criminal charges can also be filed with prosecutors. In 2012, more than 40 cases led to findings of guilt, leading to fines in excess of USD 847 million. The number of investigations and findings of guilt has been increasing.

In terms of direct contribution, the results from BRIAS have been limited: only three cases initially identified by BRIAS have led to findings of guilt. In part, this is attributable to the fact that the capacity to investigate is limited, and cases based on voluntary reporting or challenges by other suppliers begin with a more firm investigative basis than the circumstantial red flag generated by BRIAS. But during the period of its operation, voluntary reporting by cartel participants has increased significantly, and some of this increase is attributed to the raised awareness and fear of being caught generated by the implementation of the BRIAS system. This result is consistent with the OECD Recommendation on Public Procurement, which identifies the publication of risk management strategies, including systems for generating red flags, as an important element of their effectiveness.

To further expand the benefits of the BRIAS system, the FTC established a committee between project commissioners (including PPS and other large enterprises) to try to encourage adoption of a similar system at other public enterprises. In addition to providing the same functionality in a broader range of public procurement cases, spreading systems like this will allow the FTC to develop broader expertise, based on the differences in procurement practices at different entities, to better identify and prosecute cases of collusion. Dissemination activities are also undertaken to spread awareness and identify typical cases of collusion. In addition, the PPS training centre recently developed a separate training course on collusion, implemented in collaboration with the FTC.

Box 1.7. **Public Spending Observatory in Brazil**

The Office of the Comptroller General of the Union launched the Public Spending Observatory (*Observatório da Despesa Pública*) in 2008 as the basis for continuous detection and sanctioning of misconduct and corruption. Through the Public Spending Observatory, procurement expenditure data are cross-checked with other government databases as a means of identifying atypical situations that, while not *a priori* evidence of irregularities, warrant further examination.

Based on the experience over the past several years, a number of daily actions are taken to cross procurement and other government data. This exercise generates "orange" or "red" flags that can be followed up and investigated by officials within the Office of the Comptroller General of the Union. In many cases, follow-up activities are conducted together with special Advisors on Internal Control and internal audit units within public organisations.

Examples of these tracks related to procurement and administrative contracts include possible conflicts of interest, inappropriate use of exemptions and waivers and substantial contract amendments. A number of tracks also relate to suspicious patterns of bid-rotation and market division among competitors by sector, geographic area or time, which might indicate that bidders are acting in a collusive scheme.

Finally, tracks also exist regarding the use of federal government payment cards and administrative agreements (*convenios*). In 2013, there were 60 000 instances of warnings originated from the computer-assisted audit tracks used by the Office of the Comptroller General of the Union to identify possible procurement irregularities, like:

1. business relations between suppliers participating in the same procurement procedure
2. fractioning of contracts in order to use exemptions to the competitive procurement modality
3. non-compliance by suppliers with tender submission deadlines
4. registration of bid submissions on non-working days
5. supplier's bid submissions or company records with the same registered address
6. contract amounts above the legally prescribed ceiling for the procurement modality used
7. contract amendments within a month of contract award, in violation of the specific tender modality
8. evidence of bidder rotation in procurement procedures
9. use of reverse auctions for engineering services
10. micro- and small-sized enterprises with shareholders in other micro- and small-sized enterprises
11. personal relations between suppliers and public officials in procurement procedures
12. use of bid waiver when more than one "exclusive" supplier exists
13. bid submission received prior to publication of a procurement notice
14. possibility of competition in exemptions
15. participation of newly established suppliers in procurement procedures
16. contract amendments above an established limit, in violation of the specific tender modality
17. commitments issued prior to the original proposal date in the commitment registration system
18. bidding procedures involving suppliers registered in the Information Registry of Unpaid Federal Public Sector Credits (*CadastroInformativo de CréditosNãoQuitados do SetorPúblico Federal*)
19. micro- and small-sized enterprises linked to other enterprises
20. micro- and small-sized enterprises with earnings greater than BRL 0.24 million or BRL 2.40 million, respectively.

Source: OECD (forthcoming), *Compendium of Good Practices for Integrity in Public Procurement.*

Finally, additional work is underway to improve the function of the BRIAS system. While this sort of system of generating red flags will always generate only circumstantial indications of potential collusion, the FTC is conducting an ongoing evaluation of the formula and indicator elements to improve accuracy. In addition to adjustments for increased accuracy, monitoring of the formulas involved in this sort of system and changing them over time is necessary to address changes in the market. Collusion presents an evolving fight, as cartels adjust their practices to adapt to new means of identifying bid rigging.

Key findings and recommendations

The Korean public procurement system, viewed through the role and responsibilities of PPS, is a high functioning and mature public procurement system. At its centre, the system is defined through a coherent and stable legal and regulatory framework. Such a framework is necessary for ensuring fair access to public procurement opportunities for all potential competitors, as recognised in Element IV (i) of the OECD Recommendation.

As a centre of efficiency, PPS serves the role of a central purchasing body, and implements many good practices consistent with Element VII (iii) of the OECD Recommendation, which encourages countries to "develop and use tools to improve procurement procedures, reduce duplication and achieve greater value for money, including centralised purchasing, framework agreements, e-catalogues." The success of PPS in effectively implementing this recommendation is demonstrated by the fact that use of PPS' purchasing services continues to increase, despite the fact that mandatory use of these services by local and other entities has been phased out over time.

This increased use, along with reports of satisfaction from users of the wide variety of PPS' services, indicates that PPS offers a value proposition for the end user, demonstrating implementation of Element VII (ii) of the OECD Recommendation to "implement sound technical processes to satisfy customer needs efficiently." The adoption of a revolving budget account to facilitate prompt payment of suppliers, the availability of a call centre to address technical questions from end-user buyers and suppliers, and the general efficiency of the Online Shopping Mall experience are all evidence of success in this area.

In general, necessary training opportunities are available, consistent with Element IX of the OECD Recommendation, though more could be done to co-ordinate trainings offered by various sources. As in some other civil service systems, a rotational assignment policy is implemented to foster integrity, consistent with Element III (ii) of the OECD Recommendation: "implement general public sector integrity tools". This process poses some challenges for the professionalisation of the public procurement function, but these challenges can be addressed through the further development of the procurement certification programme and the development of a network of public buyers to share information and resources.

Finally, the oversight functions of the PPS Audit Office, the BAI and the FTC are appropriately identified to ensure co-ordination and limited overlap, consistent with Element XII (iv) of the OECD Recommendation. The PPS Audit Office provides appropriate attention to *ex ante* monitoring processes, including both standard system monitoring and specific attention to high-risk contract actions. Information necessary for the actions of BAI is provided as needed from the KONEPS data warehouse. As part of its activities to identify collusion and bid rigging, the FTC continues to develop a red flags system to identify suspicious cases. Publication of this risk management strategy appears to be generating additional results in the form of self-reporting by cartel members concerned about being caught. These actions are good examples of implementation of Element XI of the OECD Recommendation, which encourages integrated risk management through the development of tools and the publication of such strategies.

Summary of recommendations for action

- Better co-ordinate training offerings to compliment and supplement other available training.
- Examine procurement certification programmes to establish relevant and meaningful benefits for public procurement officials who obtain certification.
- Develop a network of public buyers as a forum for communication, collaboration and information dissemination. This network can also serve a knowledge management function, over time, as shared information is collected.
- Develop client management files and appropriate outreach protocols for transfer of responsibility.
- Consider integration of audit findings with regular curriculum development for training activities, to better incorporate lessons learned.

Notes

1. Values in this report have been converted from KRW to USD using a rate of 0.0084763 USD per KRW, obtained on 15 September 2015. In some cases, data were originally presented in USD; these cases are identified with appropriate endnotes.
2. The costs for training were originally provided in USD.

References

Federal Ministry of the Interior (2014), "Rules on integrity", www.bmi.bund.de/SharedDocs/Downloads/EN/Broschueren/2014/rules-on-integrity.html.

OECD (forthcoming), *Compendium of Good Practices for Integrity in Public Procurement.*

OECD (2015a), *Government at a Glance 2015*, OECD Publishing, Paris, http://dx.doi.org/10.1787/gov_glance-2015-en.

OECD (2015b), "Recommendation of the Council on Public Procurement", www.oecd.org/corruption/recommendation-on-public-procurement.htm.

Public Procurement Service (2013), "2013 annual report: Public Procurement Service, the Republic of Korea", www.pps.go.kr/eng.

Chapter 2

Driving efficiency through e-procurement: KONEPS

A central responsibility of the Public Procurement Service (PPS) involves management of the Korean ON-line E-Procurement System (KONEPS), which involves both policy and purchasing dimensions. KONEPS processes nearly two-thirds of all public procurement in Korea, and responsibility for the system is undertaken in an integrated and strategic manner, driving continuous improvements for public procurement. Within this context, the present chapter presents an analysis of the e-procurement experience in Korea, centred on the Korea ON-line E-Procurement System (KONEPS). As an integrated system developed over many years, KONEPS offers many lessons for countries considering the development or expansion of e-procurement tools and systems. By examining the history, functions and capacities of KONEPS, these good practices are identified, as are recommendations and considerations for additional improvements.

The use of digital technology to support procurement processes dates from the second half of the 20th century as a way to improve automation and standardisation, reducing time to complete tasks and the probability of human error. With the gradual expansion of capacities and systems in the last 30 years, its use enlarged to progressively cover more areas of the procurement cycle, until it became commonly known as e-procurement. At the same time, the use of digital technology in the public sector has been a strategic driver for improving efficiency and supporting effectiveness of policies by creating more open, transparent, innovative, participatory and trustworthy government. In this light, the use of e-procurement not only increases efficiency by facilitating access to public tenders - increasing competition and decreasing administrative burdens - but can also improve transparency by holding public authorities more accountable.

This essential twofold role for e-procurement is recognised in the 2015 OECD "Recommendation of the Council on Public Procurement" (hereafter, the "OECD Recommendation") (Box 2.1).

Box 2.1. **OECD Recommendation on e-procurement**

VII. RECOMMENDS that Adherents improve the public procurement system by harnessing the use of digital technologies to support appropriate **e-procurement** innovation throughout the procurement cycle.

To this end, Adherents should:

i) Employ recent digital technology developments that allow integrated e-procurement solutions covering the procurement cycle. Information and communication technologies should be used in public procurement to ensure transparency and access to public tenders, increasing competition, simplifying processes for contract award and management, driving cost savings and integrating public procurement and public finance information.

ii) Pursue state-of-the-art e-procurement tools that are modular, flexible, scalable and secure in order to assure business continuity, privacy and integrity, provide fair treatment and protect sensitive data, while supplying the core capabilities and functions that allow business innovation. E-procurement tools should be simple to use and appropriate to their purpose, and consistent across procurement agencies, to the extent possible; excessively complicated systems could create implementation risks and challenges for new entrants or small and medium-sized enterprises.

Source: OECD (2015a), "Recommendation of the Council on Public Procurement", www.oecd.org/corruption/recommendation-on-public-procurement.htm.

In their most straightforward application, e-procurement tools have the potential to dramatically increase efficiency by eliminating wasteful and duplicative paper-based processes. Beyond this, e-procurement tools can also play a transformative role by enabling processes that are simply impossible to replicate without advanced digital technologies. This dual potential is therefore identified in the OECD Recommendation's definition of e-procurement as "the integration of digital technologies in the replacement or redesign of paper-based procedures throughout the procurement process."

In this latter role, a well-functioning e-procurement system can advance many of the other elements of the OECD Recommendation. By providing and consolidating public procurement information, e-procurement systems foster transparency throughout the procurement cycle. Through some process automations, the need for interaction between public and private actors can be significantly reduced, eliminating some risks of corruption and fostering integrity. By ensuring that procurement opportunities are provided electronically, in standard forms, with clear information regarding the terms of award and any exceptions to competition, fair access to procurement opportunities can be achieved. Well-constructed e-procurement systems can eliminate barriers to the pursuit of secondary policy objectives in public procurement (for example, through simplifying procedures for small and medium-sized enterprises, or allowing for more innovative means of dividing consolidated procurements into regional lots to facilitate local procurement). Establishing e-procurement as part of a broader e-government programme can lead to better integration of procurement in budgeting and public finance management. Finally, the data that can be collected and generated by a comprehensive e-procurement system supports a host of other important procurement functions, including ongoing performance evaluation of the system and its outcomes, the development and deployment of risk-management strategies, and internal and external accountability.

Furthermore, in many countries, the adoption of e-procurement tools and systems has been a key driver of public procurement reform in recent years and plays a strategic role for e-government implementation plans.

History

As with many mature e-procurement systems, the current state of KONEPS is the result of a long series of evolutions. Beginning in the 1990s, public entities with large procurement volumes in Korea, including the Public Procurement Service (PPS), the Defence Acquisition Programme Administration and the Korea Electric Power Corporation began the establishment of individual e-procurement systems. While these independent systems drove some improvements in efficiency for suppliers, the multiple systems also gave rise to concerns about a lack of standardisation, the need for redundant investment, and a lack of a single portal and information-sharing capabilities. Duplication of effort was still required, resulting in unnecessary costs and inconvenience. Additionally, these individual systems still left many smaller public procurement entities relying on paper-based processes and face-to-face interactions with suppliers.

To address these issues, PPS prepared an e-procurement master plan and began the establishment of the Procurement Electronic Data Interchange (Procurement EDI) in 1996. Completed and piloted in 1999, Procurement EDI enabled the shared use of procurement-related information among PPS, other public buyers and business firms. By 2001, the application of Procurement EDI expanded to cover the entire span of procurement procedures, leading to reduced processing times, many fewer paper-based transactions and reduced payment lead times for suppliers.

As Procurement EDI was implemented, separate efforts to develop e-bidding and e-payment systems were also underway. A pilot homepage for e-bidding was launched in September of 2000, allowing bidder registration and the issuance of e-signatures. Full operation began in early 2001, and spread throughout the government purchasing offices. The e-payment system was launched in June 2001, replacing the mailing of treasury checks with electronic account transfer (EFT) payments for suppliers.

While each of these new, individual systems yielded efficiency gains and savings, gaps remained in consistent application. Public entities continued to develop their own proprietary e-procurement systems, leading to an absence of consistent, government-wide standards.

In addition, those entities that did not develop e-procurement systems still relied heavily on paper-based processes to address the elements of e-procurement not captured by the existing PPS systems. These issues arose as Korea undertook a broad and substantial e-government project, and development of a comprehensive, national e-procurement platform was selected as one of 11 national digitisation projects (see Box 2.2). This project, initially dubbed "the G2B Project," imagined a "single window" to public procurement, built around Internet-based work processes. System implementation work was awarded to a private sector developer in early 2002, and completed under the direction of PPS in September of that year: KONEPS was launched (see Figure 2.1).

Box 2.2. **E-government project in Korea**

The Ministry of Government Administration and Home Affairs (MOGAHA) is responsible for overall e-government management in Korea, including the preparation of e-government policies, instructions and guidelines, with technical support from the National Information Society Agency. The responsibilities of MOGAHA include:

- establishing policy instructions and technical standards on informatisation projects
- identifying needs for e-government projects
- assigning budgets
- monitoring and evaluating e-government projects
- evaluating informatisation performance of central government entities.

As part of these responsibilities, MOGAHA identified 11 broad projects in three categories.

- Innovation in services:
  - government-wide e-procurement system
  - single window for civil services
  - integrated social security information system
  - Internet-based national taxation system
- Administrative productivity:
  - national finance system
  - integrated administration system for local governments
  - nation-wide educational administration system
  - standardised human resources management system
  - consolidation of e-document exchange and e-reporting
- Infrastructure:
  - e-authentication and e-signature system
  - government-wide information technology (IT) governance environment

The approach adopted by the Government of Korea to design and support the implementation of the e-procurement system as part of its e-government efforts is in line with the OECD Recommendation on Digital Government Strategies (adopted by the OECD Council in July 2014). As parts of its guidance on strengthening government capabilities to ensure returns on IT investments, the OECD Recommendation calls for governments to procure digital technology based on existing assets. Additionally, the OECD Recommendation underlines the necessity to align individual strategies, such as the e-procurement strategy, with digital government strategies to ensure they all support coherently overarching policy goals and public sector reform agendas (e.g. fostering more efficient public sectors, increasing transparency, promoting competitiveness and growth by providing fair opportunities).

Source: PPS response to OECD internal questionnaire, 2014 with updates in 2015.

Figure 2.1. **KONEPS development: Before and after**

Source: PPS response to OECD internal questionnaire, 2014 with updates in 2015.

KONEPS scope of functions and usage

KONEPS is a comprehensive, full-fledged e-procurement system covering the entire procurement cycle, including procurement requests from public buyers, publication of tender notices, communication with suppliers, collection of e-bid submissions, bid opening and contract award, inspection and e-payment. From its launch in 2002, KONEPS has been regularly updated to expand its functionalities: an intelligent product information search and implementation of an online shopping mall came in 2006, mobile e-bidding services were added in 2008, radio-frequency identification (RFID)-based inventory management was added in 2009, and fingerprint recognition e-bidding was added in 2010 (Public Procurement Service, 2013). A detailed list of the functions appears in Table 2.1.

Given this wide range of functions, KONEPS is in the forefront of e-procurement systems in terms of scope and coverage, even when compared to other OECD country systems. In fact while the use of e-procurement systems in the form of portals or websites among OECD member countries is pervasive, when moving along the procurement cycle the role actually played by e-procurement in public procurement processes is reduced. As of 2014, all OECD member countries announce procurement opportunities and provide tender documents through their e-procurement systems; most of these countries are mandated by law to provide these functionalities. Functionalities at the beginning of the procurement cycle - in particular publishing of procurement plans (86%), electronic submission of bids (90%), and e-tendering (86%) - are provided in most OECD countries. In contrast, those towards the end of procurement cycle (except for notification of award [97%]) are provided by a lower number of OECD member countries. Fewer countries provide e-auctions, ordering, electronic submission of invoices and *ex post* contract management through their e-procurement systems. It is worthwhile to mention that the majority of countries provide these functionalities in their e-procurement systems even though they are not obliged by law (Table 2.2).

Table 2.1. **KONEPS functions**

Subsystem	Functions
E-procurement portal	• Comprehensive user guide on KONEPS, including user manual, downloadable resources, announcements, FAQ, Q&A, etc. • User-customised information on "My Page" after logon • Consolidated tender information
User management system	• Registration and approval of master user information on public entities and private firms • Registration of e-certificates issued by certification agencies as part of user information • Management of private firms' status with regard to sanctions imposed for illicit practices: entry suspension and lifting of debarment • Secure logon using e-certificate
Product catalogue system	• Search products by product classification, name or specifications • Classification request for products to be newly registered
E-surety system	• Receipt of e-surety through data interchange with surety companies, for bid bond, performance bond, payment guarantee, and guarantee against defects • Entry of surety information, for surety companies without electronic surety information management system
Supplier information management system	• Collection of bidder information including financial standing, past experiences, and possession of technology or quality related certificates • Checking information on licensed engineers and experts, through data interchange with industry associations
E-bidding system	• Publication of advance notice for preliminary specifications, review and receipt of feedback from private firms • Publication of pre-qualification notice for public works tenders / application for pre-qualification / processing of prequalification results • Publication of tender notice (with issuance of encryption and decryption keys for information security) • Search for tender notice, submission of e-bid (encrypted before submission) • Electronic signing of Bidding Consortium Agreement • Online negotiation for direct contracts • Opening of e-bids and determination of order of priority for contract awarding • Eligibility test (pass-or-fail evaluation for contractor candidate, based on price factors and non-price factors) • Determination of contract awardee and real-time publication of bidding details and results
E-contracting system	• Drafting and e-contract and transmission to contract awardee • Review and acceptance/denial of draft e-contract by contract awardee • Electronic signing and transmission of e-contract
E-payment system	• Contract information review • Request for upfront payment • Request for inspection (for delivery of goods, completion of public works) and response • Checking inspection result • Submission of payment request • Receipt of payment request and payment approval
Online Shopping Mall	• Product search by product category, name, and other properties • Placing products into shopping cart • Generation and transmission of online order form • Management of order information
E-document distribution and external data interchange system	• Security module management for e-certificate (e-signature) • E-document security based on public key infrastructure (PKI) encryption standards • Authenticity check for documents issued • Management of data interchange with external data systems • Management of all electronic documents between end-user public buyers and suppliers using KONEPS

Source: PPS response to OECD internal questionnaire, 2014 with updates in 2015.

Table 2.2. **Functionalities provided in e-procurement systems**

	Mandatory and provided	Not mandatory but provided	Not provided
Publishing procurement plans (about forecasted government needs)	AUS, BEL, CHL, DMK, GRC, HUN, IRL, KOR, MEX, NZL, NOR, PRT, GBR, USA	AUT, CAN, FIN, DEU, ITA, JPN, POL, SVN, ESP, SWE, CHE	EST, FRA, LUX, SVK
Announcing tenders	AUS, AUT, BEL, CAN, CHL, DNK, EST, FIN, FRA, DEU, GRC, HUN, IRL, ITA, KOR, LUX, MEX, NZL, NOR, POL, PRT, SVK, SVN, ESP, SWE, CHE, GBR, USA	JPN	
Provision of tender documents	AUS, AUT, BEL, CHL, EST, FIN, FRA, DEU, GRC, HUN, IRL, KOR, MEX, NZL, NOR, POL, PRT, SVK, SVN, SWE, CHE, GBR, USA	CAN, DNK, ITA, JPN, LUX, ESP	
Electronic submission of bids (excluding by e-mails)	BEL, CHL, EST, FRA, GRC, ITA, MEX, PRT, USA	AUS, AUT, CAN, DNK, FIN, DEU, IRL, JPN, KOR, LUX, NZL, NOR, SVK, SVN, ESP, SWE, GBR	HUN, POL, CHE
E-tendering	BEL, CAN, CHL, EST, GRC, IRL, ITA, MEX, CHE, USA	AUT, DNK, FIN, FRA, DEU, JPN, KOR, NZL, NOR, PRT, SVK, SVN, ESP, SWE, GBR	AUS, HUN, LUX, POL
E-auctions (in e-tendering)	GRC, MEX, SVK, SVN, USA	DNK, EST, FIN, FRA, DEU, IRL, ITA, NZL, NOR, PRT, SWE, CHE, GBR	AUS, AUT, BEL, CAN, CHL, HUN, JPN, KOR, LUX, POL, ESP
Notification of award	AUT, BEL, CAN, CHL, DNK, EST, FIN, DEU, GRC, HUN, IRL, KOR, MEX, NZL, NOR, POL, PRT, SVK, SVN, ESP, SWE, CHE, USA	AUS, FRA, ITA, JPN, GBR	LUX
Ordering	CHL, FIN, ITA, CHE, USA	AUT, BEL, CAN, DNK, FRA, DEU, JPN, KOR, NZL, NOR, SVN, ESP, SWE, GBR	AUS, EST, GRC, HUN, IRL, LUX, MEX, POL, PRT, SVK
Electronic submission of invoices (excluding by e-mails)	AUT, DNK, FIN, ITA, ESP, SVN, SWE, CHE, USA	FRA, DEU, JPN, KOR, NZL, NOR, GBR	AUS, BEL, CAN, CHL, EST, GRC, HUN, IRL, LUX, MEX, POL, PRT, SVK
Ex post contract management	CHE, USA	AUT, DNK, FIN, DEU, ITA, JPN, KOR, NZL, NOR, SWE	AUS, BEL, CAN, CHL, EST, FRA, GRC, HUN, IRL, LUX, MEX, POL, PRT, SVK, SVN, ESP, GBR

Source: OECD (2015b), *Government at a Glance 2015*, OECD Publishing, Paris, http://dx.doi.org/10.1787/gov_glance-2015-en.

By offering comprehensive coverage of the procurement cycle and by allowing public entities to use the system in an independent manner, KONEPS managed to represent the most significant portion of the Korean public procurement market. In fact, total public procurement in Korea amounted to USD 95.8 billion in 2013, of which USD 61.6 billion, or 64.3%, was transacted through KONEPS. This amount represents the maintenance of the upsurge trend from 2011, while still far from the USD 72.9 billion registered in 2009 (Table 2.3).

Table 2.3. **KONEPS share in total procurement volume**

In USD billions

	Transaction volume		Percentage
	Total volume	KONEPS volume	
2009	103.4	72.9	70.5%
2010	88.5	63.7	71.9%
2011	84.6	54.1	63.9%
2012	90.2	56.5	62.7%
2013	81.2	61.6	64.3%

Source: PPS response to OECD internal questionnaire, 2014 with updates in 2015.

The number of transactions through KONEPS is split almost evenly between PPS and other public entities and has been growing steadily. In the past ten years the number of transactions of both type of users doubled, which reflects a wider recognition and usage of the system (see Figure 2.2).

Figure 2.2. **Transactions through KONEPS**

In USD billions

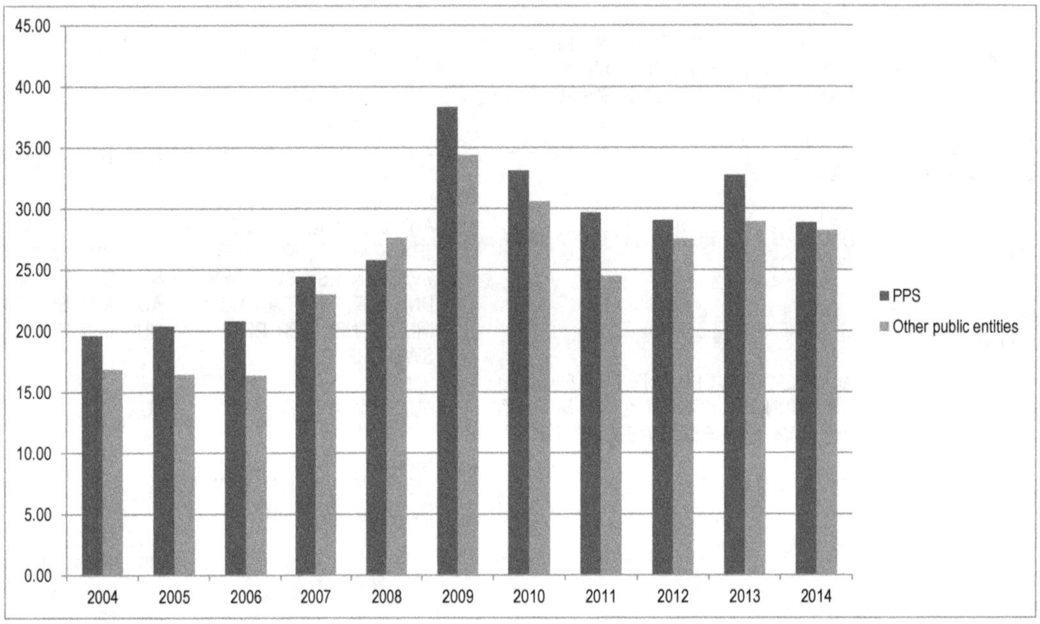

Source: PPS response to OECD internal questionnaire, 2014 with updates in 2015.

The 48 000 buying entities that use KONEPS come from central government, local governments, educational entities and public enterprises (see Figure 2.3).

Registration has also increased steadily over time, more than doubling the number of public entity and private firm users in ten years to approximately 48 000 and 290 000, respectively (see Figure 2.4), with more than 560 000 individual user accounts registered. Some 200 000 users log on daily, and a similar number of e-documents are processed on a daily basis. In 2014, there were 20 million bids on approximately 240 000 biddings conducted through KONEPS.

The KONEPS Online Shopping Mall provides a catalogue of more than 360 000 product models with capabilities for purchasers to order directly, and discounted quotations can be requested for orders larger than USD 42 400. In 2014, USD 11.4 billion were processed as orders through the Online Shopping Mall, representing 60% of PPS purchasing of goods and services. For other goods and services (for example, those not available in the Online Shopping Mall, or in circumstances where particular terms or specifications are required), contracts are handled through KONEPS in the form of fixed-price contracts issued through e-bidding (Table 2.4).

Figure 2.3. **Public entity users by type**

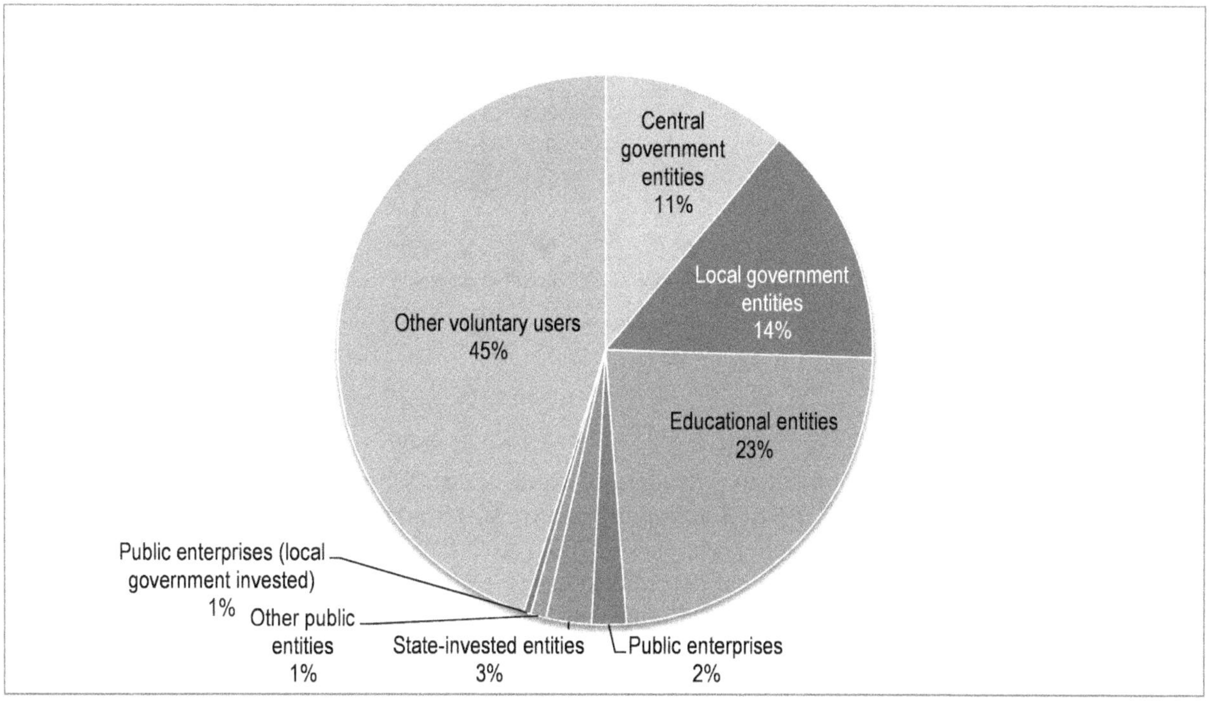

Central government entities 11%
Local government entities 14%
Educational entities 23%
Public enterprises 2%
State-invested entities 3%
Other public entities 1%
Public enterprises (local government invested) 1%
Other voluntary users 45%

Source: PPS response to OECD internal questionnaire, 2014 with updates in 2015.

Figure 2.4. **Number of KONEPS users**

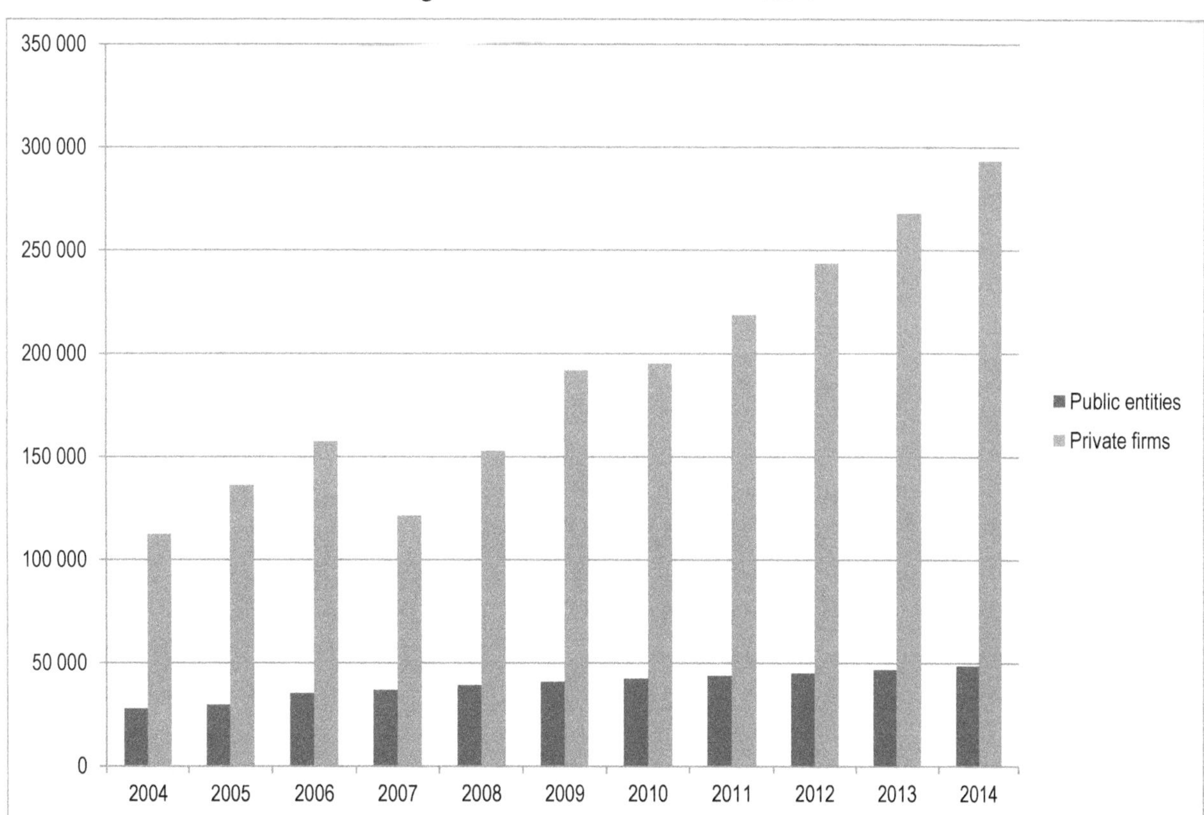

350 000
300 000
250 000
200 000
150 000
100 000
50 000
0
2004
2005
2006
2007
2008
2009
2010
2011
2012
2013
2014
Public entities
Private firms

Source: PPS response to OECD internal questionnaire, 2014 with updates in 2015.

Table 2.4. **Transactions via KONEPS**

In USD billions

		2010	2011	2012	2013	2014
Central procurement	Lump-sum contract	24.3	20.4	18.4	20.9	17.4
	Online Shopping Mall	8.8	9.3	10.6	11.8	11.5
	Total	33.1	29.7	29.1	32.7	28.9
Autonomous procurement by public buyers		30.6	24.4	27.5	28.9	28.2
Total		63.7	54.1	56.6	61.7	57.1

Source: PPS response to OECD internal questionnaire, 2014 with updates in 2015.

KONEPS outcomes

Efficiency

Central to this ability to standardise and centralise functionalities is the interconnection between KONEPS and many diverse electronic systems, both within and outside the government's reach. At launch in 2002, KONEPS contained digital interfaces for data exchange with 50 external database systems. Over time, this network has grown to more than 160 interconnected digital systems (see Figure 2.5). In addition to connection with other e-procurement systems to allow seamless sharing of bid and tender information, these connections cover a broad range of information types, each allowing for additional efficiency, reduced duplication and cost savings.

Figure 2.5. **Data connections in KONEPS**

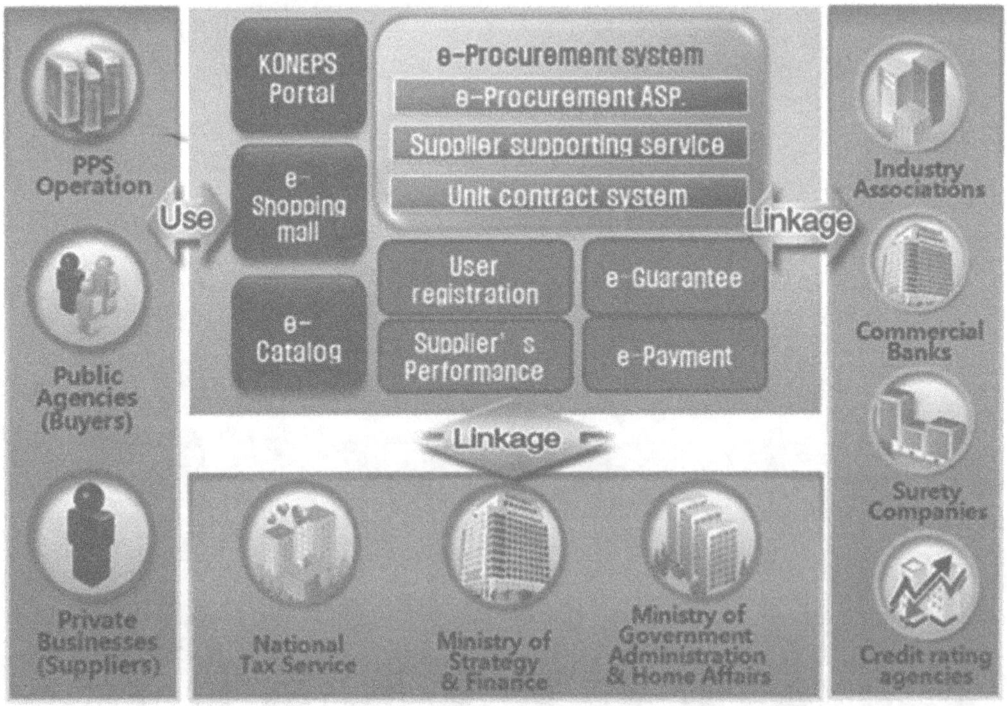

Source: PPS response to OECD internal questionnaire, 2014 with updates in 2015.

Connection with 19 surety companies allows automated verification of four types of sureties, including bid bonds and performance bonds. Interfaces with 12 private sector associations and 9 credit ratings companies allows for the automatic collection of credit and past performance data, which is used to verify qualifications and evaluate bids. There are 15 commercial banks connected for e-payment through EFT, and also for processing loans that are available to support government contract holders. Business registration certificates and tax-payment certificates are transmitted through appropriate data exchange interfaces. In addition to collecting information from external sources, information from KONEPS is also shared with 28 public entities and 34 private sector information systems.

As a result of this integration, 477 document forms used in public procurement, including bid forms, contract forms, inspection requests and payment requests, have all been converted to digital equivalents. In addition to the increased efficiency of processing all of these transactions and procurement steps electronically, bidders are no longer required to visit public authorities to collect and submit – to each public buying entity separately – the documentation necessary for participation in public procurement. This results also in increased transparency, as the information is available on line through KONEPS, as well as increased access for new entrants and small and medium-sized enterprises, as the burden to participate in public procurement is much smaller.

A description of these work-process benefits divided by relevant parts of the procurement cycle is presented in Table 2.5, allowing a direct comparison of the changes introduced by the system.

Table 2.5. **Work process comparison**

Phase	Before KONEPS	After KONEPS
Bidder registration	Businesses register individually for each bidding in which they intend to participate.	Businesses are able to participate in any bidding from public entities after a one-time registration with KONEPS.
Procurement request	Procurement requests are prepared on paper and submitted to public entities.	Procurement requests are prepared through KONEPS and submitted on line.
Tender notice	Tenders were advertised in the government's official gazette and newspapers.	All tenders are advertised through the KONEPS portal.
	Businesses obtained tender information individually from each public entity, often through subscriptions to private services.	Businesses obtain all public sector tender information from KONEPS.
Bid submission and bid opening	Bids are submitted in person or via post, and opened at a designated place.	Bids are submitted on line, and opened through the contracting official's computer.
Contracting	Contracts are prepared and sealed in paper, with attached paper documents.	Contracts are prepared and processed on line (including modifications), and digitally sealed with an e-certificate.
Invoicing	Inspection requests and invoices are prepared manually and submitted on paper.	Inspection requests and invoices are prepared through KONEPS and submitted on line.

The introduction of KONEPS also fostered efficiency and delivered value for money. A study conducted by Hanyang University in 2009 indicates that these changes led to an estimated USD 8 billion[1] in annual transaction-cost savings (see Table 2.6) – primarily in savings to the private sector in reduced costs for visiting public entities, obtaining required certificates and proof documents and registering and updating accounts in multiple systems.

Table 2.6. **Estimated transaction-cost savings enabled through KONEPS**

In USD millions

	Central government entities	Local government entities	Public enterprises	PPS	Total
Public sector	123.8	872.4	166.3	58.5	1221.0
Private sector	826.9	4074.6	691.0	11.4	5603.9
Total	950.7	4947.0	857.3	69.9	6824.9

Source: PPS response to OECD internal questionnaire, 2014 with updates in 2015.

The value of KONEPS in creating efficiency is supported by interviews with stakeholders. Both buying agency representatives and individuals from companies registered as sellers on KONEPS reported satisfaction with the ease and functionality of the system. One interview subject commented that, despite the fact that his volume of business in public procurement has grown dramatically since the introduction of KONEPS, the staff required to process the work has remained relatively constant, thanks to the efficiency benefits of the system.

Recommendations on efficiency

Some room for improvement remains, as indicated in interviews with both buying agencies and from the supplier perspective. Some buyers reported that, while generally a very good system, improvements could be made to the search functions included in KONEPS. Three specific areas were mentioned, all related to the ease of use of the Online Shopping Mall. First, the search function does not allow users to filter by social objective (for example, local procurement or small and medium-sized enterprise), which sometimes makes the process more complicated for buyers who are trying to satisfy social objective goals. Next, the text-based search logic was reported to require somewhat specific search terms (for example, "Freezing and refrigerating device for…" when searching for refrigerators), and this could be improved to generate more relevant results from simpler search terms. Finally, one buyer requested better or more detailed classification by groups, to make browsing through the hundreds of thousands of items in the Online Shopping Mall more effective. On the supplier side, the recommendation was similar with regard to searching through tender opportunities: a progressive filtering option would make the interface more user-friendly for suppliers.

One additional recommendation concerns a functionality that is present in KONEPS, but currently unutilised: the ability to conduct electronic auctions. In the procurement context, electronic auctions can be used to drive savings by providing bidding vendors an opportunity to offer more favourable prices in real time. While there are mechanisms in the Multiple Award Schedules (MAS) framework contracts and the Online Shopping Mall processes that serve to ensure prices are adjusted downward as the market changes, implementation of the electronic auctions module could drive increased savings. But electronic auctions could yield even greater savings in the procurements currently conducted via e-contracting in KONEPS, outside of these two frameworks.

Integrity and security

The system also serves to enhance the integrity of the public procurement system through the adoption of digital processes, as face-to-face interactions and other opportunities for potential corruption are reduced through the centralised and automatic transfer of data between systems. To support integrity, KONEPS operates digital encryption and decryption based on PKI encryption, and utilises time-stamping to prevent access to bidding data prior to authorised bidding times.

Additional recent enhancements to KONEPS further address the concern that illegal practices and collusive acts could be caused by borrowed e-certificates. In order to mitigate this risk, the Public Procurement Service introduced "Fingerprint Recognition e-Bidding" in 2010. In the Fingerprint Recognition E-bidding System, each user can represent only one company by using a biometric security token. Fingerprint information is stored only in the concerned supplier's token, thus avoiding any controversy over the government's storage of personal biometric information. By July 2010, it was applied in all tenders carried out via the E-Procurement System by local governments and other public organisations for procuring goods, services and construction projects (OECD, 2013).

As a further innovation, PPS has implemented a virtual desktop application to ensure the safety of the e-bidding environment. Going beyond the need to protect KONEPS itself, the adoption of the virtual personal computer system is designed to address the concern that the security environment varies among users, and that procurement data such as bidding information could be vulnerable to interception via malware prior to transmission to KONEPS. By downloading and utilising the virtual PC environment, tender officials and participating bidders create a logical separation between the physical PC being used to run the system and the virtual PC environment that is used to operate KONEPS and transmit data. This is accomplished through a complete simulation of the PC environment, including the encrypting key bid information, which is run independently from the physical PC. Operating KONEPS through the virtual PC system provides an additional efficiency benefit, as the system is optimised for KONEPS and can be used on any system capable of installing the virtual PC system, eliminating the need to address differences in user hardware. Overseen and managed by the National Computing and Information Agency, mandatory use of the enhanced virtual security system is now in place for all tender notifications through KONEPS. As of July 2015, 94% of participating bidders are using the enhanced system, and plans are underway to expand to those bids still published by individual end-user entities.

These developments have led to an increase in public trust in the procurement process. The National Integrity Commission of Korea conducts a regular integrity survey of public entities, and the integrity index for PPS rose by 27.2% between the launch of KONEPS in 2002 and 2005.

Transparency and data

The degree of transparency in public procurement in Korea has also been greatly expanded by KONEPS. Real-time disclosure of tender notices, bidding details and results, awarding information and contracting information is now available. On a per-contract level, the general public can track the history of each transaction, from tendering through to invoicing. Publication of all tender notices through KONEPS also allows for ready comparisons of terms and conditions, and tenders published by PPS also require a five-to-seven-day advertisement for preliminary specification review. This period allows for challenges to tenders that may contain unnecessarily restrictive terms and conditions, which fosters fair and open competition. Such challenges and any responses are also publicly available.

This increased data collection and consolidation also yields benefits for strategic planning and accountability. Public buyers have access to procurement records to a degree that allows tracing of prices and specifications over time, as well as price-trend information that can be used to structure future contracts or procurement plans. Additionally, the KONEPS statistics module generates reports for a variety of relevant purposes. Specifically, the module can provide buying entities with insights into such things as the use of various contract types (fixed contracts, unit price, etc.), proportion of central vs. independent contracts, and progress toward social objective goals. Data is also readily available to satisfy external reporting requirements, including reporting to the Small and Medium Business Administration (SMBA) and the Board of Audit and Inspection of Korea (BAI) that is required for oversight purposes.

Recommendations on transparency and data

While the progress made in this area is quite substantial, there are still some gaps that can be addressed through further development. One example is the reporting required to the SMBA regarding the buying agency's progress toward satisfaction of procurement goals for social objectives. SMBA is required by law to report this information, and procurement entities are therefore required to report this information to SMBA. This process currently involves retrieving the relevant information from within KONEPS, combining that information with data held by the procuring agency regarding micro-purchases and other sources, and manually transmitting the information to the SMBA. In other cases, agencies that operate their own e-procurement systems (and use KONEPS primarily for tender notices, as required by law) maintain their own data. This multi-step process is currently necessary because KONEPS cannot capture these external sources of data.

This is a clear case where additional co-operation and data integration could serve to simplify the reporting required by SMBA by further reducing duplication, burden and the possibility of error that comes with manual data entry and transmission. Additionally, expansion to include all sources of procurement information would serve to allow for better and more consistent reporting regarding public procurement in Korea as a whole, without requiring manual inputs to produce such information. An effort is underway to address these issues through the creation of a Public Procurement Data System; more information on this initiative is presented below.

The large collection of information available within KONEPS could also be more extensively used to measure performance through the development and deployment of procurement metrics and indicators. There are certain performance measures that apply across the civil service in Korea (for example, the integrity survey mentioned above), but none that are specific to public procurement. Savings are calculated according to an internal PPS mechanism based on the detailed establishment of reference prices, with general savings of 2% to 9% reported, but this information does not feed into any consolidated reporting. While KONEPS can provide detailed information regarding, for example, how many bidders are participating in tenders, this and other internal monitoring elements are not tracked and reported as official indicators of public procurement performance, either for individual buying agencies or for the system as a whole.

Indicators of this sort, if developed, could provide insights into trends over time, for instance regarding market changes that could lead to a need to develop new procurement approaches. If combined with better integration of various existing data systems, as recommended above, such indicators could also provide a means of comparing performance across different public buyers with different procurement systems, eventually driving improved performance through better sharing of best practices or evidence to support the use of KONEPS and PPS for those agencies that currently chose not to do so.

KONEPS management

KONEPS was developed and implemented by an external supplier, but an effort is underway to centralise the management of KONEPS within PPS. In the original implementation of KONEPS, the prime contractor conducted operations in five main areas, though much of the work was done in partnership with subcontractors. PPS conducted an 18-month planning process, and the desired goal is to internalise core processes related directly to tendering and award selection. Different private partners now head the four other areas.

Any transition of this sort involves risks, some substantial, to the continuity of operations of the system. PPS managed the most meaningful risks by arranging a gradual reduction of the role of the original prime contractor and maintaining several of the subcontractors operating in the prior agreement. Additionally, PPS will recruit five public employees and seven contract-based employees as part of the first phase of the transition. Ensuring appropriate management and skills is crucial, both in terms of ensuring continued and effective service, and in achieving the right balance between contractor support and internal capabilities to manage the system, as indicated by the US example of inherently governmental and critical functions (see Box 2.3).

Given the complex network of connections between KONEPS and other systems, change management is another area that warrants careful attention. The system operates according to well-defined data standards and interfaces, but changes are sometimes necessary (examples could include the collection of a new data field, a change to an electronic form that is used by more than one entity, or the creation of new forms for reporting or transfer of data). When new data is required, the process varies depending on whether the affected system is a public entity system or an external system. The public entities connected to KONEPS have a consulting group that governs changes, so the relevant stakeholders meet to agree to the necessary changes. For external entities like banks, credit-rating companies and industry associations, KONEPS has individual Memoranda of Understanding with each entity, so a change requires that the terms be changed on a one-by-one basis for the affected systems.

The implementation and management of e-procurement systems is an ongoing effort in OECD member countries and the challenges they face are common and need to be understood in order to be addressed successfully. The KONEPS implementation process has been running for over 12 years now and many challenges faced during this period are also present in some other countries. When responding to the OECD Survey on Public Procurement, the main challenge faced by both procuring entities and potential bidders and suppliers to use e-procurement systems are low knowledge and skills of information and communications technology (ICT) (48%) and that is still today the case of Korea. Low innovative organisational culture (41%) and low knowledge of the economic opportunities raised by e-procurement systems (32%) were identified as additional challenges for procuring entities. Related to potential bidders and suppliers, 12 OECD member countries (41%) identified difficulties in understanding or applying the procedures and difficulties in the use of the functionalities as additional challenges (see Table 2.7).

Box 2.3. Inherently governmental and critical functions in the United States

As governments rely more heavily on contractors to provide services in support of policy development and citizen-facing activities, risks arise that functions properly belonging to the government may be undertaken or unduly influenced by private sector suppliers. To address these risks, the United States Congress directed the Office of Management and Budget to:

i) create a single definition for the term "inherently governmental function" that addresses any deficiencies in the existing definitions and reasonably applies to all agencies

ii) establish criteria to be used by [US federal government] agencies to identify "critical" functions and positions that should only be performed by federal employees

iii) provide guidance to improve internal agency management of functions that are inherently governmental or critical (§321, Pub. L. 110-417)

To implement this direction, the Office of Management and Budget, through its office of Federal Procurement Policy, issued a policy letter to better identify such situations and provide guidance regarding the management of internal staffing decisions to ensure critical management roles are filled by federal employees or members of the Armed Forces.

The policy letter unified existing definitions of the term "inherently governmental functions," which are defined as a function that is so intimately related to the public interest as to require performance by Federal Government employees. According to the policy letter, this term includes functions "that require either the exercise of discretion in applying Federal Government authority or the making of value judgments in making decisions for the Federal Government, including judgments relating to monetary transactions and entitlements." Specific examples such as binding the government by contract, engaging in policy making, and managing officers or employees of the government are also included. The term normally excludes gathering information or providing policy advice and functions that are primarily ministerial and internal, such as building security and mail operations.

While inherently governmental functions cannot be performed by contractor employees, contractors are eligible to perform functions closely associated with inherently governmental functions, subject to certain conditions. When the nature of a function that is not inherently governmental but may impinge on federal officials' performance of inherently governmental functions, agencies are required to give special consideration to using federal employees to conduct the function. In cases where contractors are used to conduct such functions, special management attention is required on the part of the agency to guard against expansion into a role in performing inherently governmental functions. The policy letter includes examples of closely associated functions, as well as a checklist of responsibilities for management of contractors performing functions closely associated with inherently governmental functions, including contractual provisions to limit discretion, appropriately identifying contractor work as such when there is a risk of confusion with government work products, and maintaining sufficient and effective management and oversight of contractor performance.

The policy letter defines a critical functions as "a function that is necessary to the agency being able to effectively perform and maintain control of its mission and operations. Typically, critical functions are recurring and long-term in duration." Due to the mission-oriented nature of this definition, whether a function is critical or not can vary by agency, but some examples are provided – for instance, performing mediation services for the Federal Mediation and Conciliation Service. The policy letter requires that agencies identify such functions "in order to ensure that they have sufficient internal capacity to maintain control over functions that are core to the agency's mission and operations."

While critical functions may be performed by contractor personnel (as long as they are not also inherently governmental), the policy letter requires that agencies have an "adequate number of positions filled by Federal employees with appropriate training, experience, and expertise to understand the agency's requirements, formulate alternatives, manage work product, and monitor any contractors used to support the Federal workforce" with respect to critical functions. This determination should be based on a number of case-by-case factors, including the agency mission, complexity of the function, the need for specialised staff, and the potential impact on mission performance of a default of performance by the contractor.

Source: Office of Federal Procurement Policy, (2011), "Policy Letter 11-01, Performance of inherently governmental and critical functions," Office of Management and Budget, www.gpo.gov/fdsys/pkg/FR-2011-09-12/pdf/2011-23165.pdf.

Table 2.7. **Main challenges to the use of e-procurement systems**

	Procuring entities				Potential bidders/suppliers					
	Low knowledge/ ICT skills	Low knowledge of the economic opportunities raised by this tool	Low innovative organisational culture	Do not know	Low knowledge/ ICT skills	Low knowledge of the economic opportunities raised by this tool	Difficulties to understand or apply the procedure	Difficulties in the use of functionalities (e.g. catalogue management)	Low propensity to innovation	Do not know
Australia	No major challenges faced by procuring entities				No major challenges faced by potential bidders/suppliers					
Austria				•						•
Belgium			•						•	
Canada	•				•	•	•	•	•	
Chile				•		•	•	•		
Denmark				•			•	•		
Estonia		•				•				
Finland				•						•
France				•						•
Germany	•	•	•			•		•		
Greece		•	•		•	•			•	
Hungary	•		•		•		•	•		
Ireland				•			•			
Italy	•		•		•		•	•	•	
Japan	•	•			•	•	•	•		
Korea	•		•		•				•	
Luxembourg				•						•
Mexico	•	•	•							•
New Zealand	•	•			•	•				
Norway		•				•	•		•	
Poland	•		•		•		•	•		
Portugal	•				•		•			
Slovak Republic		•			•			•		
Slovenia	•	•	•		•	•	•	•	•	
Spain		•	•		•	•			•	
Sweden				•						•
Switzerland				•						•
United Kingdom	•		•			•		•		
United States	•		•		•		•	•	•	
Brazil	•	•	•		•	•	•	•		
Colombia	•	•	•		•	•			•	
OECD 29	13	10	12	9	13	11	12	12	9	7

Source: OECD (2015b), *Government at a Glance 2015*, OECD Publishing, Paris, http://dx.doi.org/10.1787/gov_glance-2015-en.

Additional innovations and next steps

Subcontract Management System for Government Contracts (SMSGC)

As in many country contexts, there were concerns in Korea regarding the treatment of subcontractors by government contract holders. While project owners are legally required to approve subcontracts, following an examination of the propriety and payment price, there was little transparency into the realities of subcontracting practice because most of these processes are conducted manually. This led to reports of a number of practices including post-award demands for price reductions, delayed payments or non-payment, and the use of dual contracts, one presented to PPS and another drawn up to represent the actual arrangement at less favourable terms to the subcontractor.

To address these issues, PPS established the SMSGC to allow project owners to more effectively manage the subcontracting process consistently and effectively. As with many elements in KONEPS, these benefits are largely realised through the elimination of manual processes throughout the entire subcontracting cycle, through payment to suppliers. The system came on line in December of 2013, and PPS is currently engaged in efforts to expand its use through promotional activities and trainings. For construction works and IT projects facilitated by PPS, project owners are recommended to include use of SMSGC as one of the terms of the contract. In addition, promotional video clips were developed and shared in major transit, online newspaper and social media venues.

After one year of operation, these efforts are showing results, with 588 public organisations (more than half of those conducting construction works valued at more than USD 1 million or software projects valued above USD 300 000 registered in the SMSGC system. The system was utilised in 772 projects valued at approximately USD 5.6 billion, dramatically exceeding the initial target of USD 2.7 billion for the initial deployment.

Given that many construction subcontractors, materials suppliers and IT companies are small and medium-sized enterprises, progress in ensuring proper payment – both on time (see Table 2.8) and the right amount - and the elimination of dual contracts serves as an additional and innovative way to support these communities. Digital management of these processes also provides another source of additional market data that can be used to better plan and conduct large procurements, over time.

Table 2.8. **Payment time improvement for subcontractors**

Types of payment		Legal deadline (A)	Average days taken through SMSGC (B)	Shortened days (A)-(B)
Subcontract payment	Progress payment	15 days	1.5 days	13.5 days
	Advance payment	15 days	4.3 days	10.7 days
Payment for construction material		15 days	1.3 days	13.7 days
Labour cost		2 days	0.8 day	1.2 days

Source: PPS response to OECD internal questionnaire, 2014 with updates in 2015.

Transfer of these functions to a digital system, which no longer requires an in-person review of subcontracting arrangements, is also projected to save more than USD 14 million per year in staff labour costs, if fully implemented across the public sector. To that end, PPS is working to amend the Act on the Use and Promotion of

Electronic Procurement to require the use of SMSGC for large construction and IT projects.

Opening KONEPS services to the private sector

While the adoption of e-procurement through KONEPS drives substantial efficiencies in public sector purchasing, many non-profit and small or medium-sized enterprises still conduct their own purchasing through paper-based processes. Even for those private sector entities that can justify the cost of implementing an e-procurement system for their own purchases, it is an investment cost that could be spent elsewhere, if an alternative existed.

The Act on Use and Promotion of Electronic Procurement of 2013 provided PPS with legal authority to begin allowing private entities to use KONEPS services for their procurement processes. Beginning with a pilot programme, this option launched in October of 2013 as KONEPS bidding services were opened for apartment complex management offices and farming and fishing cooperatives through a designated section within KONEPS. In 2014, the programme was further opened to non-profit entities. The development of standardised forms for private sector e-procurement occurred in June of 2014, and standard contract conditions were published in September of that year. To drive further expansion, a separate KONEPS system for private entities was launched in January 2015. Processing the entire e-procurement cycle, from e-contracting, pre-qualification, reverse auctions and e-invoicing, the system is expected to be available for use by up to 3.35 million small and medium-sized businesses (see Table 2.9).

Table 2.9. **Implementation plan for opening KONEPS services to the private sector**

	2013	2014	2015
Target	Apartment complexes, Farming and fishery cooperatives	Non-profit entities	Small and medium-sized enterprises
	30 000	10 000	3 350 000
Process	E-bidding	-	E-contract, e-invoicing
The status of openness	Test	First expansion of openness	Second expansion of openness, Establishment of a separate KONEPS system for private entities

Source: PPS response to OECD internal questionnaire, 2014 with updates in 2015.

While participation by private sector entities is voluntary, promotion and education activities about the web-based procurement system are underway to raise awareness of the benefits that the system can bring for eligible small and medium-sized businesses. A variety of channels are being used to promote awareness, including press releases, public interviews with the Korea Broadcast System, newspaper contributions and subway advertisements, the development and distribution of an e-procurement guidebook and promotion events.

To date, 246 training sessions on procurement have been conducted for approximately 6 800 trainees. To target specific relevant sectors, training is offered at relevant meetings, such as training for apartment management officers at the general meeting of the Korean Housing Manager's Association. These efforts are showing results, as 439 e-biddings have been conducted through the system through December of 2014 with more than 3 209 private entities participating. Competition in these biddings was strong, with an average of 7.8 suppliers per bid, and savings are estimated at 10.7% (amounting to USD 11 867).

Aimed at reducing administrative costs in procurement transactions across the country while increasing transparency and standardisation, this innovation has the potential to drive inclusive growth by levelling the playing field for private sector procurement. By reducing or eliminating the need for private sector entities, particularly small and medium-sized enterprises, to engage in inefficient and duplicative paper-based processes, this option will reduce the need for duplicative investments in conversion to e-procurement society wide, allowing additional capital to be better deployed in growing and developing those businesses.

Public Procurement Data System

While almost 70% of public procurement transactions occur via KONEPS, the remaining transactions, including defence procurement, procurement transactions by other public enterprises that use their own e-procurement systems and some manual transactions, are not currently captured in a centralised way. In 2013, PPS launched a Public Procurement Data System project to close this gap and provide policy makers and citizens with complete procurement transaction data across the entire public sector, enabling a better understanding of the procurement market and an analytical study on the policy results.

Proper legal authority for the project was established by the modifications of procurement laws including the Government Procurement Act (July 2013) and the Enforcement Decree on the Government Procurement Act (January 2014), giving PPS the legal authority to request data and establishing deadlines for government agencies to submit the requested procurement data.

Total public procurement encompasses procurements that occur in both electronic and non-electronic ways. Electronic procurement is carried out on KONEPS and 23 other electronic procurement platforms for specific procuring entities. Thus, data integration includes linking of the 24 e-procurement systems as well as central collection of manual records. A report will be prepared to present the data collected per government bodies, companies, and projects. Data will also be presented in infographics in order to facilitate end user comprehension.

The data integration faces some difficulties due to administrative burdens that are imposed on approximately 28 000 government agencies and delays in concomitant projects in some government agencies to improve their electronic systems, which were intended to facilitate the data integration. In order to alleviate the administrative burden on the collection of manually kept data, discussion on linking with other financial information systems is taking place, including the Educational Financial System, the Local Government Budget and Accounting System, the Local Pubic Enterprise Budget and Accounting System and the National Budget and Accounting System. Additionally, some difficulties arose due to the disparity of the information collected at each government agency and across different e-procurement systems. In response, new code mapping was provided to agencies where data were collected by different standards.

Provision and publication of data statistics on total public procurement on a monthly and annual basis and 103 specific reports based on the data are expected to increase availability of the data for companies and the public, and enhance transparency of the government budget. The reports will be made available on line.

Public Procurement Freight Information System for Government Commodities

In an effort to better utilise procurement data to further drive efficiency, PPS is pursuing the public disclosure of transportation data for government-contracted commodities. While more than 1 million public procurement contracts are conducted on an annual basis, there is currently no co-ordination of the logistics and shipping information related to these contracts. By sharing this information through a Public Procurement Freight Information System for Government Commodities, PPS would link freight information with the vehicle arrangement details of carriers, with the goal of reducing the freight carrier empty transfer rate.

As of May 2015, PPS is implementing a feasibility study to analyse the practices of the logistics industry in how information is collected on potential cargos, how such information is used for business operations, and how data on public contracts and scheduled deliveries could be effectively utilised. Combining original public contract data with additional details such as supply date, transportation, departure and arrival information, the goal is to enable long-term logistical planning. Open access to transportation information will be provided from June 2015, with the goal of establishing the full system between 2016 and 2017.

Key findings and recommendations

As an extensively developed e-procurement system, KONEPS contributes substantially to the efficiency, effectiveness and integrity of public procurement in Korea. In addition to these many contributions, additional developments are continuously underway to drive improvement. Beyond improvements to the public procurement system, continued expansion to allow use of KONEPS by private sector buying entities demonstrates Korea's commitment to driving investment and inclusive growth, especially among small and medium-sized enterprises.

KONEPS satisfies all of the components of Element VIII of the OECD Recommendation by providing an integrated e-procurement system that addresses all phases of the procurement cycle. Transparency is provided through the collection and publication of public procurement information, and access for vendors and other stakeholders is assured not only through standardised and simplified processes, but also through regular trainings and the availability of a help desk that is readily available to answer questions about the use of the system.

The "modular, flexible, scalable and secure" development required by Element VIII (ii) of the OECD Recommendation is also evident. Developed over time, KONEPS is continually improved through the addition of new functional modules. In addition to the historical development, this ability to adapt the system to new demands from public procurement stakeholders is evidenced by innovative new features such as providing KONEPS services for private sector purchasers. The commitment to security is demonstrated through the use of encryption and digital fingerprint technologies.

Providing this kind of simple, ready access also facilitates competition by lowering the barriers to entry for suppliers and other public procurement stakeholders. To this end, KONEPS serves to implement Element IV (ii) of the OECD Recommendation: "Deliver clear and integrated tender documentation, standardised where possible and proportionate to the need." In addition to standardising many processes, which facilitates access by a broad range of participants, KONEPS implements tools that help ensure that "the extent and complexity of information required in tender documentation and the time allotted for suppliers to respond is proportionate to the size and complexity of the procurement."

The development of KONEPS also addresses Element VII of the OECD Recommendation, by implementing "processes to drive efficiency throughout the public procurement cycle in satisfying the needs of the government and its citizens." By creating a single online portal for the posting of public procurement opportunities, KONEPS "streamline[s] the public procurement system and its institutional frameworks," by reducing the need for duplicative systems in other institutions. Increased use by other buying entities despite the removal of mandatory use requirements demonstrates success in developing "a more service-oriented public procurement system… built around efficient and effective procurement processes and workflows to reduce administrative red tape and costs."

KONEPS also collects "consistent, up-to-date and reliable information and use data on prior procurements," consistent with Element X (i) of the OECD Recommendation. This data, combined with the other information that is available in or linked from KONEPS, serves to "promote fair and equitable treatment for potential suppliers by providing an adequate degree of transparency in each phase of the public procurement cycle," (Element II [i] of the OECD Recommendation) and is publicly available, as appropriate, consistent with Element II (ii). It is also used for regular monitoring of the system's functioning, as discussed in the previous chapter. Next steps in this area include further data integration with the other e-procurement systems operated in Korea, and to begin using the volume and variety of information available to develop more sophisticated procurement metrics and indicators to monitor the health and efficiency of the public procurement system.

The data collected by KONEPS also supports Element XII of the OECD Recommendation by allowing the application of "oversight and control mechanisms to support accountability throughout the public procurement cycle." Complaints from suppliers are tracked from within KONEPS, and the outcome is publicly available, consistent with Element XII (iii). As discussed in the previous chapter, the availability of data from KONEPS supports internal and external controls and audits as required by Element XII (iv). Finally, the transparency of KONEPS and other features such as the elimination of many points of face-to-face contact between public procurement officials and suppliers is an expression of Element III(ii), implementing "general public sector integrity tools and tailoring them to the specific risks of the procurement cycle as necessary."

KONEPS implementation also provides an example of good practice in areas that go beyond the OECD Recommendation. Implemented as part of a broader e-government development, the approach adopted by Korea is in line with the OECD Recommendation on Digital Government Strategies. Aligning the individual e-procurement strategy with digital government strategies ensures that they support and complement coherently overarching policy goals and public sector reform agendas (e.g. fostering more efficient public sectors, increasing transparency, promoting competitiveness and growth by providing fair opportunities).

Finally, the recent expansion of KONEPS to allow for use by private sector suppliers demonstrates an innovative approach to using public procurement to support inclusive growth and investment. Providing access to KONEPS functionality has the potential to dramatically increase efficiency for small and medium-sized businesses, by eliminating the need for burdensome paper-based procurement processes or the need to purchase and implement an individual e-procurement system. This savings in resources can instead be used to further grow and develop small and medium-sized businesses, which are a critical component of the Korean economy.

Given the many strengths of KONEPS, the recommendations for action primarily address future developments and additional considerations that could be implemented. While there were some requests from buyers and suppliers regarding improvements to the search functions, most feedback regarding the functioning of KONEPS was very positive.

Summary of recommendations for action

- Improve KONEPS Online Shopping Mall search functionality for public buyers. Specifically:
  - The ability to filter searches by social objectives should be added to facilitate the achievement of social goals through public procurement.
  - The text-based search logic should be improved to generate better results when using natural language searching.
  - To the extent possible, more detailed hierarchies by category should be created to allow for a more convenient browsing experience of the items available in the Online Shopping Mall.
- Improve KONEPS tenders search functionality for suppliers. A progressive filtering option to narrow down open tenders by type, requirements for social category, etc. would be helpful for suppliers looking to identify relevant tender opportunities.
- Activate the dormant electronic auctions function within KONEPS. Even if only deployed in some cases of procurement requests that led to open tenders, electronic auctions have the ability to drive cost savings if used appropriately.
- Implement the Public Procurement Data System to improve procurement data collection and centralisation. Procurement data should be collected and centralised in a manner that eliminates the need for manual transmission and entry of statistics to satisfy reporting requirements.
- Building on this improved centralised data, develop procurement metrics and indicators to monitor the health and efficiency of the public procurement system.
- Continue to apply careful risk-management approaches as operation of the KONEPS system transfers from a private supplier to in-house control.

Note

1. This figure was originally reported in USD.

References

Office of Federal Procurement Policy, (2011), "Policy Letter 11-01, Performance of inherently governmental and critical functions," Office of Management and Budget, www.gpo.gov/fdsys/pkg/FR-2011-09-12/pdf/2011-23165.pdf.

OECD (2015a), "Recommendation of the Council on Public Procurement", www.oecd.org/corruption/recommendation-on-public-procurement.htm.

OECD (2015b), *Government at a Glance 2015*, OECD Publishing, Paris, http://dx.doi.org/10.1787/gov_glance-2015-en.

OECD (2013), *Implementing the OECD Principles for Integrity in Public Procurement: Progress since 2008*, OECD Public Governance Reviews, OECD Publishing, Paris, http://dx.doi.org/10.1787/9789264201385-en.

Public Procurement Service (2013), "2013 annual report: Public Procurement Service, the Republic of Korea", www.pps.go.kr/eng.

Chapter 3

Supporting competition and savings through framework agreements: Multiple Award Schedule contracts

An important mandate for the Public Procurement Service (PPS) involves the operation of framework agreements – contracts containing set terms from which individual orders can then be placed. Framework agreements are an important driver of efficiency in public procurement, allowing for reduced administrative duplication as well as potential savings from centralised purchasing. This chapter presents the PPS implementation of the Multiple Award Schedules (MAS) system of framework agreements, including a detailed look at their current function and future directions.

Among the tools for delivering efficiency through public procurement, many countries are adopting and expanding the use of centralised purchasing. This change in purchasing behaviour can serve a number of purposes. By purchasing commonly used goods or services centrally, substantial administrative savings can be generated through the elimination of duplicative procurement practices. Standardisation of goods purchased by a government can also reduce costs for maintenance or related goods, as spare parts or additional materials (for example, printer toner) are also standardised. Perhaps most importantly, purchasing centrally can allow for the aggregation of demand, providing access to price discounts due to economies of scale that cannot be realised if each entity purchases on its own.

Framework agreements, which involve awarding contracts containing set terms from which individual orders are then placed, can serve many of the same benefits. For frequently purchased goods and services, a framework agreement can reduce administrative costs for both public purchasers and suppliers by allowing simplified ordering processes once the agreement is in place. Depending on the nature of the framework agreement, the benefits of aggregating demand and standardising models can also be realised. If structured to allow second stage competition, where multiple holders of a contract under a framework agreement compete to receive orders by offering discounts on the stated price, additional cost savings can be generated.

The importance of these two tools for increasing the efficiency of the public procurement process is recognised in the OECD "Recommendation of the Council on Public Procurement" (hereafter, the "OECD Recommendation") (see Box 3.1).

Box 3.1. **OECD Recommendation on efficiency**

VII. RECOMMENDS that Adherents develop processes to drive **efficiency** throughout the public procurement cycle in satisfying the needs of the government and its citizens.

To this end, Adherents should:

…

iii) **Develop and use tools to improve procurement procedures, reduce duplication and achieve greater value for money,** including centralised purchasing, framework agreements, e-catalogues, dynamic purchasing, e-auctions, joint procurements and contracts with options. Application of such tools across sub-national levels of government, where appropriate and feasible, could further drive efficiency.

Source: OECD (2015), "Recommendation of the Council on Public Procurement", www.oecd.org/corruption/recommendation-on-public-procurement.htm.

History of the Multiple Award Schedules (MAS) system

While unit-price and lump-sum contracts had been issued by Public Procurement Service (PPS) for many years, there was a recognition that a lack of diversity among goods offered through such contracts was not providing an effective solution, because it limited the options for end-user public buyers. An attempt was made to take better advantage of the existing contracts by implementing an automated process called the Multi-goods Supplying System in 2001. This system selected multiple suppliers in the order of lowest price, but the same limitations on the end users' options resulted from an insignificant quantity of contracted goods and a lack of diversity among those goods. For this reason, the system was abolished.

To address the issue, PPS undertook research of the arrangements for framework agreements in several countries with developed public procurement systems. The US Multiple Award Schedules (MAS) programme was studied in August of 2003; framework agreements in the United Kingdom were examined in May of 200; and the Canadian standing offer system was researched in July of 2004. On the basis of this research, a legal foundation for the implementation of Korea's MAS was implemented through amendment of the Enforcement Decree of the Government Procurement Act and implemented through additional related regulations (see Box 3.2). On the basis of these changes, implementation of MAS began in January of 2005.

Box 3.2. **Related laws and regulations**

Article 5 of the Government Procurement Act

The Administrator of the Public Procurement Service may enter into contracts according to the contracting methods prescribed by Presidential Decree, if he/she deems it necessary to purchase and supply demand commodities and stockpile commodities commonly required by each end user.

Article 7-2 of the Enforcement Decree of the Government Procurement Act

Where the Administrator of the Public Procurement Service deems it necessary to satisfy the diverse demand of end users when he/she purchases commodities in demand commonly required by each end user pursuant to Article 5-1 of the Act, he/she may enter into a contract for supply with two or more persons as parties to a contract so that each end user may select commodities in demand equal or similar to one another in quality, performance, efficiency, etc.

Features of MAS

Overview

MAS was designed to meet the differing needs of various end users through contracts awarded to multiple suppliers, each offering goods of similar quality, performance and efficiency. PPS issues unit-price contracts annually with qualified suppliers, who must have an acceptable past delivery performance and satisfactory financial standing. These products and prices are then listed in the Online Shopping Mall, and each end user can make purchases directly, without the need for direct involvement of PPS contracting staff or the issuance of a new contract.

This arrangement provides a number of benefits. First, it provides more options for end users by providing access to a broader range of suppliers. It also allows more suppliers to participate in the public procurement process – as long as the minimum requirements for satisfactory past performance in at least three instances and a credit rating above a certain threshold are satisfied, any supplier can participate. This increased number of suppliers also generates increased competition. Not only do suppliers compete on price, but also on quality of similar product, delivery terms and rated after-sales service, which refers to the suppliers' responsiveness to inquiries, requests for action on defects and other performance elements.

When compared side-by-side, the process to establish a MAS contract involves more complexity than the process involved in generally contracted goods and services, as illustrated in Box 3.3. However, once established, the MAS contracts provide substantial savings in the form of streamlined processes for individual orders from multiple purchasing entities.

The establishment of MAS in Korea follows international good practices in terms of tender and competition as the initial tender is always an open procedure. Several OECD and non-OECD countries have developed different models with different degrees of centralisation and usage of framework agreements, usually allied with the establishment of central purchasing bodies (CPBs), as is the case in Portugal (see Box 3.4), New Zealand (see Box 3.5) and Austria (see Box 3.6).

As of December 2014, 326 409 items were contracted with MAS, which accounts for 88.5% of total goods registered in the Korean ON-line E-Procurement System (KONEPS), totalling USD 53.9 million. This represents an increase of approximately 50% of annual value supplied since 2008. The number of contractors increased over 80% since 2008, to reach more than 5 000 (see Table 3.1). Further, small and medium-sized enterprises (SMEs) account for 98.4% of MAS contractors, which is solid evidence of the outreach of the programme. The vast majority of MAS is covering products, with different degrees of standardisation and complexity, covering a wide range of goods for many diversified uses. A list of categories covered by MAS contracts is presented in Annex A.

Box 3.3. **Generally contracted goods and services vs. MAS**

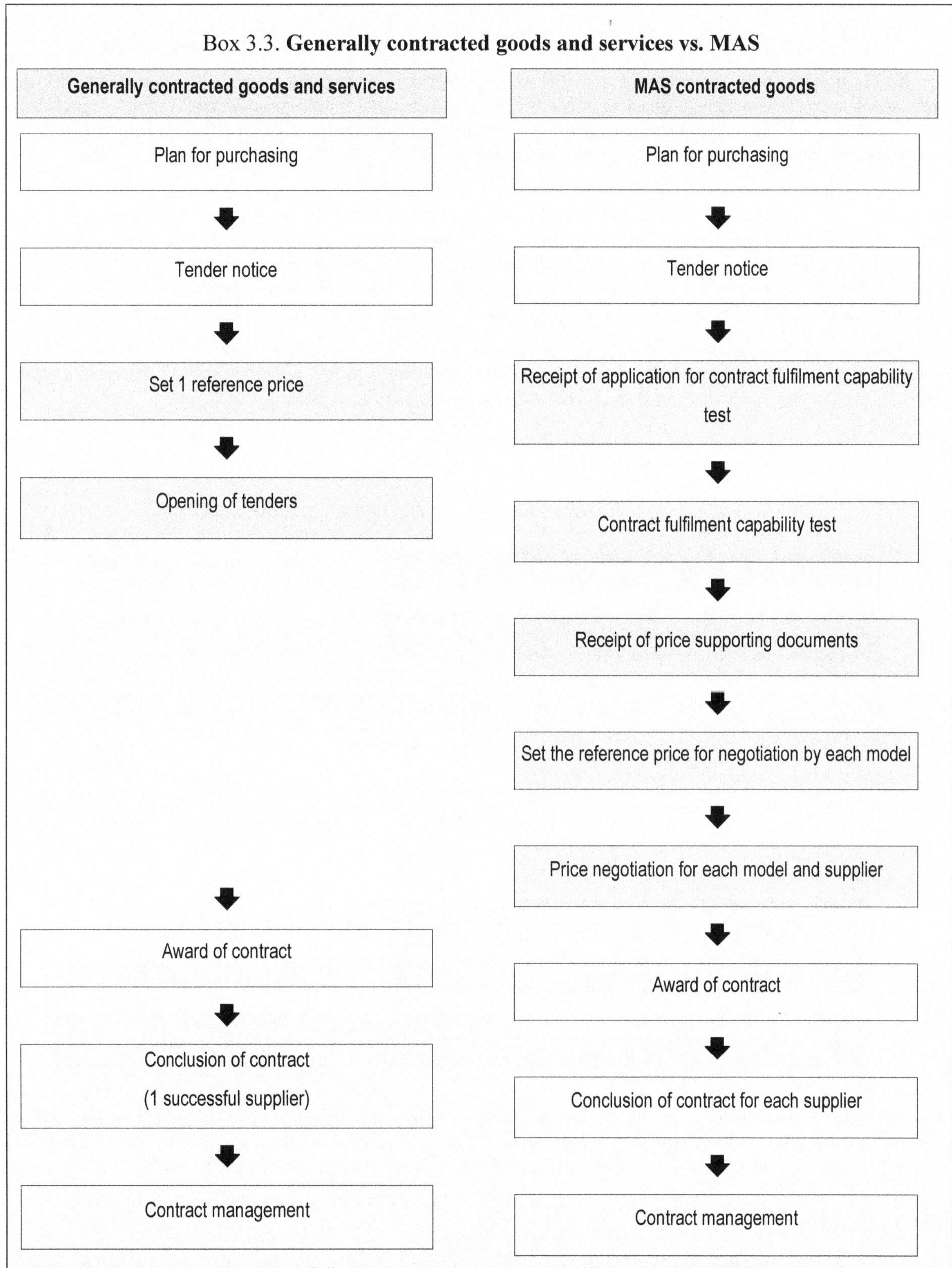

Box 3.4. **The development of framework agreements in Portugal**

The utilisation of framework agreements (FAs) by electronic means and through e-procurement was the instrument used for connecting all users into the Portuguese national public procurement system. Framework agreements are a widely used instrument within CPBs in the European Union has it privilege the principles of rationalisation, standardisation, efficiency and transparency.

The framework agreements in Portugal cover a list of transversal goods and services and call-offs are mandatory. Contracting authorities in the central administration must use the existing FA[1] to buy the items, via the existing e-catalogue, in principle using aggregation processes conducted at central purchasing units at ministerial level (UMC). Each FA has a set of rules and tender documents to facilitate the launch of the call-offs. There is also a web process to authorise specific exceptions to the use of FA, upon request from the contracting authority, given by the Agency or the Minister of Finance, depending on the type and amount of the request.

Also, the entities in the *Sistema Nacional de Compras Públicas* (SNCP) have to use the e-platform contracted by the *Agência Nacional de Compras Públicas* (ANCP) to run call-offs, free of charge, therefore allowing the Agency to better control and monitor the performance of the system.

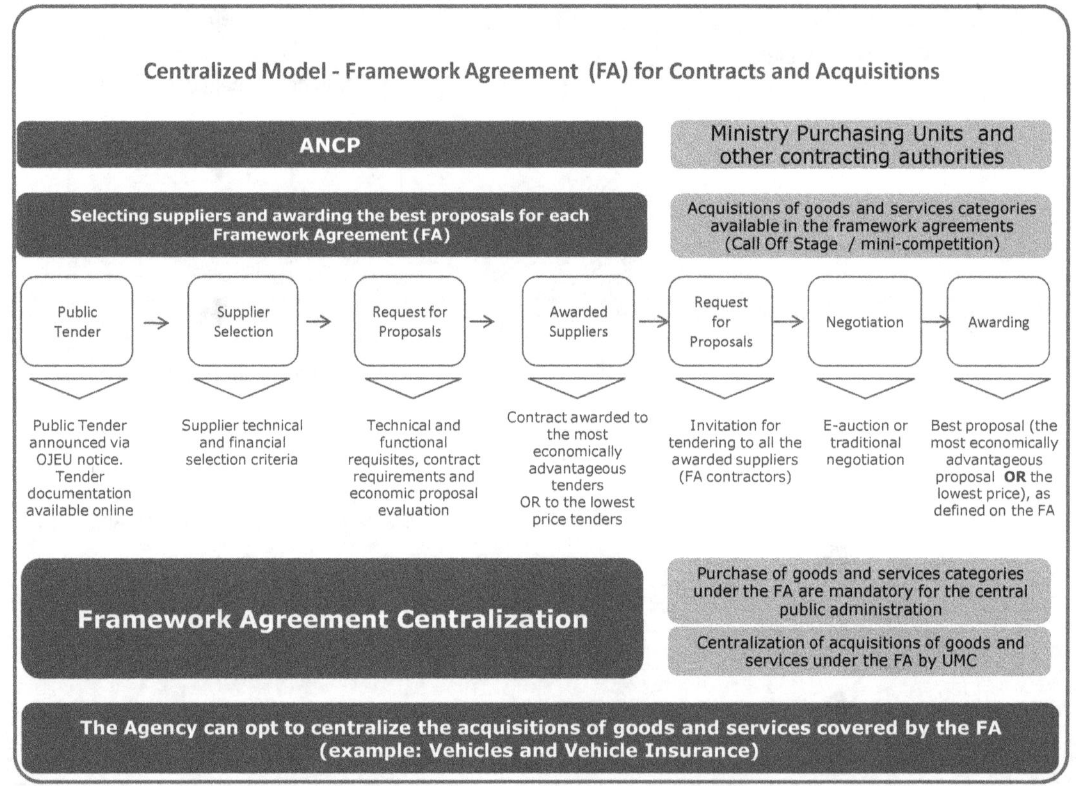

Whenever it is possible, the design of the framework agreements is done including ecological criteria, either for use in the public tender award, or during the call-off stage. Some of the FAs are included in the National Green Procurement Strategy, jointly elaborated by ANCP and by the Portuguese Agency for the Environment.

1. The definition of the categories of goods and services covered by the FA is a competence of the Minister of Finance, upon ANCP's indication.

Source: Magina, Paulo (2013), "The national public procurement system of Portugal", presentation made in Kuwait for the MENA-OECD Network on Public Procurement.

Box 3.5. **Centre-led collaborative contracts in New Zealand**

Complemented by Procurement Functional Leadership (PFL) since 2012, the Government Procurement Reform programme has been centred around three main objectives: *i)* create sound business environment for New Zealand businesses; *ii)* increase performance, add value and maximise results; and *iii)* unlock cost savings. Some key achievements of the reform programme include support for agencies to identify procurement skills gaps and areas for capability improvement, new rules for government sourcing, establishment and development of All-of-Government (AoG) contracts that have the potential to deliver cost savings and efficiencies.

A number of collaborative contracts — such as syndicated contracts, common capability contracts and AoG contracts — are managed and facilitated under the Ministry of Business, Innovation and Employment and its use has been further developed under the reform programme. Collaborative contracts allow the government agencies to achieve greater cost savings through economies of scale and produce greater value from providing consistency of policy implementation, aligning business requirements, saving transaction costs and establishing a common contract and governance framework. Recognising the potential benefits of it, an increasing number of government agencies participate in collaborative contracts. According to the PFL Progress Report of September 2014, more than 720 agencies are participating in the AoG contracts, whose number is expected to continue to grow. Total forecast savings over the lifetime of all AoG contracts have also augmented from USD 348 million to USD 415.1 million, representing in general between 10-15%.

In order to participate in an AoG contract, a government agency needs to sign a Letter of Agreement to a Memorandum of Understanding on AoG contract participation. Once the LoA is signed, the participating government agency receives a panel directory containing provider details, the primary service lots they were selected for, relative value-for-money and quality rankings, plus contracted fees. In this process, the Centre of Expertise, specialising in managing relationships and resolving issues, maintains the overall contractual relationships with each of the panel providers and government agencies maintain operational relationships with their individual panel providers (more detailed information can be found in the *AoG Buyers Guide*). The process demonstrates several benefits of the centre-led procurement process including, in addition to unlocking cost savings through aggregation of spending, improved ability to influence capability and capacity development, enforced strategic procurement and stronger centralised leadership and support.

Sources: Lyons, Grant (2013) Presentation made in Kosovo for the World Bank Workshop; Ministry of Business innovation and Employment, Government Procurement branch, www.procurement.govt.nz.

Box 3.6. **Framework agreements in Austria**

In addition to a broad range of policy responsibilities, a consulting service and the development of e-procurement applications, Austria's *Bundesbeschaffung GmbH* (BBG) is responsible for the establishment of framework agreements. As a centralised purchasing body owned by the Ministry of Finance, Austrian ministries are obligated to use the services of BBG, while the services are also available to all other contracting authorities. Purchasing volume in 2013 reached EUR 1.2 billion, with approximately 730 000 products in 12 product families available for purchase by government authorities.

In addition to evaluating government need, BBG also analyses the willingness and suitability of a given market to accept delivery through framework agreements in determining which products or services to pursue. Reference prices are determined through market analysis and historical pricing data, and framework agreements can last a maximum of three years, apart from exceptional cases where there is justification (for example, by the subject of the agreement) for an additional three years.

Austrian law provides an obligation to set out how additional competition for orders (mini-competitions) will be conducted as an element of the establishment of a framework agreement, if applicable. In cases where needs and preferred features can be clearly identified in the initial competition, the mini-competition will focus primarily on ensuring the best price. In these cases, the principle of most economically advantageous tender is used during the first stage to achieve appropriate levels of quality. In cases where some elements of the need or preferred features are not identified in the first competition, the most economically advantageous tender principle can be used during the mini-competition phase as well. While the law does not provide an explicit obligation on when and how to set the criteria for the mini-competition, experience has shown that the question is best addressed in the first phase in order to support transparency and competition most effectively.

Source: *Bundesbeschaffung GmbH*, Austria.

Table 3.1. **Annual Multiple Award Schedules performance**

	2008	2009	2010	2011	2012	2013	2014
No. of goods	240 764	297 585	273 070	297 190	300 633	305 095	326 409
No. of contractors	2 938	3 732	4 082	4 405	4 701	5 304	5 568
Total value supplied (in USD billions)	3.8	5.1	4.8	4.7	5.1	5.6	5.4

Source: PPS response to OECD internal questionnaire, 2014 with updates in 2015.

Establishment of MAS contracts

The workflow for MAS is provided in Box 3.7, and additional details about the steps in the process are provided below.

Box 3.7. **MAS workflow**

1. Plan for purchasing
   - Market research, price analysis, etc.
2. Announcement for purchasing
   - Tender notice on KONEPS
3. Receipt of application for contract fulfilment capability test
   - Past delivery performance and credit rating (checked through on line)
4. Contract fulfilment capability test
   - Evaluated by contracting division and notified on KONEPS
5. Receipt of supporting documents for price
   - Received by related contracting division (mail, e-mail or in person)
6. Set the reference price for negotiation
   - Set by related contracting division
7. Price negotiation
   - Negotiate with a qualified supplier and select a contractor
8. Conclusion of contract
   - E-contract through KONEPS
9. Request for delivery (the second stage competition)
   - End users purchase directly through KONEPS
10. Payment
    - E-payment
11. Contract management
    - Modify the contract upon contractor's request

Goods or services targeted for MAS must meet four general criteria. They must have a commercialised specification, allow for contracting via unit price, be supported by a competitive market, and have sufficient demand among end users. For goods or services that satisfy these criteria, PPS prepares an announcement for purchasing, and the tender notice is posted to KONEPS.

For most products, potential suppliers are subjected to a contract fulfilment capability test. This involves evaluation of past delivery performance and credit rating. Past delivery performance must include at least three successful contracts, though these do not need to be contracts with PPS; private sector and other public sector contracts also satisfy this requirement. Past delivery performance is rated out of 30 points. Credit rating is worth 70 points, and a credit rating of a B- equates to a score of 55 for this criterion (approximately 60% of suppliers are rated at this level). A passing score for this evaluation is 85, meaning that a contractor with a B- credit rating must receive full points for past delivery performance. In July of 2011, PPS began conducting a more thorough evaluation of suppliers for certain products (see Box 3.8).

Box 3.8. **Pre-qualification review for MAS suppliers**

As of March 2015, PPS has applied a pre-qualification review process to 18 products and services, for which quality management is deemed more important for health, safety and environmental reasons. First introduced for seven products and services on 1 July 2011, nine additional products and services were added on 1 January 2013 and two additional products were added in March of 2015. These products include: artificial grass, elastic paving materials, solar generators, non-skid paving materials, air sterilizer, air circulator, synthetic wood, stone for landscaping, bridge rails, guard rails, flooring material, urethane flooring material, water heaters, water purifiers, rock fall protection netting and lane-diving poles, natural boundary stones and median strips.

In addition to the past delivery performance and credit rating criteria, the pre-qualification review also involves an evaluation of technical capability, satisfaction rate from the post-delivery feedback from public buyers, and contractual/regulatory compliance records. For this review, a passing score is also 70, but a limited grace period of one year applies following the addition of an item to the list of those requiring pre-qualification review. During this grace period, a passing score of 65 applies. Details of the pre-qualification criteria appear in Table 3.2.

Independently of the evaluation of potential suppliers, the contracting division establishes a reference price for the subject of the MAS contract. The reference price is a hypothetical price deemed appropriate by the contracting officer for economic purchase, in consideration for the budget, the purpose of purchase, specific nature of the subject matter, and the contracting environment. This reference price acts as a ceiling price for the intended procurement, and is used as a reference in awarding contracts through bidding or negotiation. The reference price is established by the contracting official in accordance with a standard manual that reflects the appropriate legal requirements.

Table 3.2. **Pre-qualification criteria and the ceiling for allotted scores**

Classification	Allotted score	Examined area	Allotted score	Examined item	Allotted score
Total	100	Total	100	Total	100
I. Past delivery performance	20	Past delivery performance	20	Past delivery performance	20
II. Technical capability	17	Level of technology	13	High-level technology	13
				General certification	6
				Green certification	6
				Highly skilled labour force	2
		Production capacity	4	Accumulation of manufacturing technology	2
III. Credit rating	20	Credit rating	20	Credit rating	20
IV. Satisfaction rate	40	Price satisfaction	10	Price satisfaction	10
		Quality satisfaction	10	Quality satisfaction	10
		Service satisfaction	10	Service satisfaction	10
		Overall satisfaction	10	Overall satisfaction	10
V. Contractual / regulatory compliance records	3	*Ex post* management	3	Performance review of contract	3
		Reliability on contract performance	-40	Average delay on payment	-10
				Sanctions as wrongful contractors	-15
				Online Shopping Mall transaction suspension	-15

Source: PPS response to OECD internal questionnaire, 2014 with updates in 2015.

The reference price is determined through a holistic evaluation of the subject matter. Beginning with the direct price of the goods, services or works contemplated by the contract, many additional factors are considered. These include logistics costs, installation costs, necessary training costs, costs for obtaining permits, testing and inspection costs, any taxes directly associated with the procurement (for example, value-added tax, consumption taxes, education taxes, custom tariffs, or special taxes for rural development), and any other costs that need to be considered ad hoc. These additional factors are included only when they are not already considered in the direct price of the goods, services or works being procured.

Where previous transaction practices have been developed, these actual transactions are the basis of the calculation of the reference price. To survey actual transaction prices, the contracting official is instructed to survey prices published by specialised price survey institutions registered with the Ministry of Strategy and Finance, when they are available. If these are not available, the contracting official surveys two or more businesses, with information verified by tax documents, contract documents or sales ledgers.

In cases where actual transaction prices cannot be determined (for example, for newly developed products or products with particular specification requirements), the reference price is calculated through cost accounting. If there is no adequate or appropriate basis for cost accounting, reference price can be established through appraisal, transaction prices for related products, or quotations from suppliers. The priority order for these approaches is summarised in Box 3.9.

Box 3.9. **Application priority for establishing reference prices**

- price referenced in related regulations
- applicable actual transaction price
- price from cost accounting
- appraisal price
- actual transaction price for similar products (in terms of function and purpose of use)
- quotations from suppliers.

For lump sum contracts, the reference price is prepared on the total for the entire contract. For contracts where there is a continuous performance or delivery over a period of time, including MAS contracts, reference prices are prepared on a unit-price basis. In competitive tendering the contracting officials determined reference prices is considered preliminary, and the final reference price is determined through a randomising function that yields a final reference price within a percentage range of the preliminary price (the range is 2% for central government entities, and 3% for local government entities). This randomisation is conducted within KONEPS. The system generates 15 random prices within the appropriate percentage range. Each bidder for the contract then selects 2 of these 15 random prices blindly. Of those selected by bidders, the four most frequently selected are averaged to calculate the final reference price.

Once the reference price is established, PPS conducts negotiation with each approved supplier. To support this negotiation, each supplier is required to provide proof of transactions over a period of two months for each product model. This documentation is provided in the form of e-tax invoices for all MAS contracted goods; these e-tax invoices include quantities and unit prices. It is the responsibility of each supplier to download e-tax invoices from the National Tax Service and register this information on KONEPS on the 15th of every month. These registered e-tax invoices are used for the price monitoring of MAS-contracted products.

For those suppliers that reach an agreement on price negotiation, a contract is awarded. Three or more suppliers are required for a MAS contract. While MAS contracts were originally awarded for a period of one year, PPS noted that this created a burden on suppliers – and particularly on small and medium-sized enterprises – by requiring that they prepare the documents to renew the contract each year. To address this, the period for MAS contracts is now two years. Recognising that some products, such as electronics, are more vulnerable to changes in price and technological development, such products are excluded from this change, and retain one-year contract periods.

Ordering procedures

Once MAS contracts are established, the products are available within the KONEPS Online Shopping Mall. It is then the responsibility of each end user to compare, search and purchase within their needs. For simple transactions, this process is a straightforward ordering through automated processes within KONEPS. However, in certain cases there is a requirement to conduct a second stage competition for price and quality within the MAS contracting framework.

The requirements for second stage competition were introduced in 2008 in order to enhance transparency and competitiveness in larger purchases. Since March of 2012, second stage competition applies to all orders for one-time purchasing of more than USD 42 400 in the case of goods manufactured by large enterprises, and purchases over USD 84 800 for goods manufactured by SMEs. Exceptions to the requirements for second stage competition are strictly limited to cases where immediate assistance is required (for example, in response to a natural disaster) or in cases where the existing product cannot be replaced by a similar, but not identical, product because of compatibility issues.

In order to prevent public entities from avoiding this requirement by dividing the purchase into multiple smaller lots, KONEPS Online Shopping Mall is configured to track repetitive orders. If a single entity places repetitive orders for the same product and the cumulative total ordered within a rolling 30-day period exceeds the USD 42 400 or USD 84 800 threshold, the system automatically blocks further orders by the entity for the products in question.

For orders subject to second stage competition, the buying entity is required to determine evaluation criteria and request proposals from five or more suppliers. Beginning in November 2013, the system incorporates a feature whereby KONEPS automatically selects two additional suppliers at random, in addition to those selected by the buying entity, to further increase competition.

Once quotations are received, the buying entity is responsible for evaluating them according to the evaluation method selected: lowest price, standard assessment or comprehensive assessment (see Table 3.3). Based on the evaluation method selected, a period of between three to five full days is allowed for the buying entity to conduct the evaluation. In cases where a contacted supplier does not submit a proposal for evaluation, the previous contract terms and conditions are considered to be the proposal. Following evaluation and selection of the winning bidder, a request for delivery is made, and the buying entity processes payment directly through the online systems within KONEPS.

While one of the intentions of the second stage competition is to increase savings through additional competition, there is a competing concern that this pressure could cause SMEs to contract at unprofitable rates. To address this concern, PPS limits the maximum allowable discount offer to 10% for SME products. While the intention behind this limitation is virtuous, it is unclear whether a limit of 10% discount on the offered price will ultimately represent the best value for the public buyer. While some other systems enforce similar discount limits, they are often not as restrictive as 10%. For example, Portugal only blocks bids below 50% of the estimated price as unreasonably low bids. PPS should study whether this requirement is necessary, or necessarily set at this value.

Table 3.3. **Comparison of assessment methods**

	Comprehensive assessment		Standard assessment	Lowest price assessment
Items	Basic assessment (over 60 pts)	Price (45~75 pts)	o (65~75 pts)	Proposed price only
		Delivery on time (10~20 pts)	o (10~15 pts)	
		Quality inspection (5 pts)	o (5 pts)	
	Selective assessment (below 40 pts)	Technological certificate (10 pts)	o (10 pts)	
		Preference (below 5 pts)	o (5 pts)	
		Local supplier (below 5 pts)	X	
		Delivery term (below 5 pts)	X	
		Post management (below 5 pts)	o (5~10 pts)	
		Past experiences (below 5 pts)	o (5~10 pts)	
		Financial stability (below 5 pts)	X	
		Socially disadvantaged supplier (below 5 pts)	o (5 pts)	
Feature	Some assessment items can be selected by end-user public buyers		4 types of standard assessment exist, and the end-user entity may select 1 of the 4 based on their purpose of purchase	Focused on price

Contract management

MAS contracts contain provisions to ensure that the most favourable price is offered to buyers. Suppliers are only allowed to increase their prices in the case of inflation of more than 3%, pursuant to the Enforcement Decree on the Act on Contracts to Which the State is a Party. This type of raise is also only possible if at least 90 days have passed since the issuance of the contract.

Suppliers are allowed to lower the price of their products at any time. In addition, they are required to maintain a MAS price that is the most favourable price, which is determined in comparison to the market price. For this purpose, market price is the lowest price offered by the supplier to the sole distributor or its dealers, the price listed on its homepage or in catalogues, or otherwise available for purchase. In cases where a lower price is offered outside of MAS, the supplier is required to notify PPS and either adjust the price to match the lower offered price or prove that the MAS price is really the most favourable price. Exceptions apply if the difference between the market price and the PPS price is smaller than 3%, if the period of reduction in market price does not exceed 15 days (short-term sales), and as long as the number of times of price reduction is equal to or less than two times during the course of the MAS contract period. In cases where the contractor fails to voluntarily report a lower offered price for a MAS product, penalties can be applied, including the suspension of the transaction, cancellation of the contract, or debarment from future contracting for the supplier.

In cases where a supplier would like to add an additional product model to an existing contract, the contract must be revised. Such revision is allowed after 60 days have passed from the issuance of the contract, or from the most recent contract revision.

Future directions

MAS contracts for services

While most of the MAS contracts made by PPS focus on standardised commercial products, public buying has trended toward increased reliance on services, or on hybrid contracts where goods are supplied along with support services necessary for their operation. To keep pace with this trend, PPS is working to develop and expand the use of MAS contracting for services. Between 2012 and 2013, the number of services provided on MAS increased from 185 to 753. During the same period, purchasing volume increased from USD 26.6 million to USD 181.8 million.

To date, the covered services include collective insurance, mobile surveys, school field trips and other commoditised services. Building on the momentum developed in 2013, PPS established a unified service classification system to systematically increase the use of MAS contracts in service products, manage statistics, and nurture the public contracting services industries. PPS opened a designated aisle for specific services within KONEPS Online Shopping Mall in 2014, including school field trips, collective insurance and mobile surveys. Additionally, PPS has created a Service Contract Division in January of 2015 to expand MAS contracts for services.

Recommendations for expansion of MAS contracts for services

Selection for MAS contracting includes a requirement that the procured item be subject to industry-wide commercial standards and test standards. Current efforts to incorporate more services in the MAS framework contracts involve a similar effort to begin by systematically classifying services in a uniform way. While this approach will yield solid and standardised results, its application may be limited as more and more complex services are contemplated for inclusion in MAS contracts, as complex services are not always easy to characterise in a neat and standard way.

For this reason, consideration of approaches that incorporate additional flexibility may be required. For complex services, a category management approach may be necessary. Under such an approach, PPS could assemble individuals with market expertise to appropriately structure framework agreements for complex services in the absence of criteria that are easily standardised. For such cases, comprehensive evaluation during second stage competition would be necessary, as price alone would likely be a poor indicator for complex services. But this approach is applied in other OECD countries, for example, through the application of Quality Assurance Plans in France (see Box 3.10) and strategic sourcing and collaboration (see Box 3.11). As most of the current MAS contracts focus primarily on awarding to lowest cost providers, the move to services and a category management approach necessitates consideration of additional workforce skills and training. Contracting based on best value requires additional skills and experience as well as new training for the workforce.

Box 3.10. **Quality assurance plan: An example of cleaning services in France**

The *Union des groupements d'achats publics* (UGAP, Union of Public Purchasing Groups) is a French central purchasing body that buys products and services and sells them to the government and government agencies, regional authorities and hospitals. Its purchasing categories include vehicles, information technology (IT), furniture and equipment, medical supplies, maintenance and technical services and facility management services.

In 2014, UGAP concluded a framework agreement for cleaning services. The agreement has a duration of four years and is divided into 26 regional lots. For each lot, seven to ten suppliers are selected. When buyers wish to place a purchase order, they conduct a mini-tender in which suppliers submit bids to win the order, in accordance with the mini-tender award criteria defined in the framework agreement.

This agreement includes a quality assurance plan to evaluate the quality of the services rendered by the supplier and assess whether it is within specific thresholds established by UGAP. The quality assurance plan formed part of the tender documents, so bidders were aware that they would be bound to it if they won the contract.

In order to evaluate the quality of services, the quality assurance plan foresees with three different kinds of inspections of the services, to take place at agreed intervals (once a month or a trimester):

1. self-inspections carried out by the supplier
2. planned inspections carried out by the supplier and the public buyer
3. unplanned inspections carried out by the supplier and the public buyer.

For the self-inspection, the supplier has to monitor itself the quality of the services, carrying out verification operations and taking immediate corrective measures where needed. At the end of the inspection, the supplier has to evaluate the level of services according to a predefined index and is responsible for the accuracy of the information.

For the planned inspections, the buyer has to inform the supplier at least 48 hours before the inspection. At the end of the inspection, the supplier has to evaluate the level of services according to the predefined index. If the rating is under a certain threshold, the supplier has 48 hours to solve the problem and is liable for a penalty. The amounts of penalties depend on the extent of the defect in performance, i.e. their amounts increase as quality levels fall.

The unplanned inspections are carried out after an obvious worsening of the quality of the services that does not correspond to the agreed quality levels. The supplier and buyer carry out the inspection 24 hours following a demand. At the end of the inspection, the supplier has to evaluate the level of services according to the predefined index. If the rating is under a certain threshold, the supplier has 48 hours to solve the problem and is liable for a penalty.

In addition, any buyer who notices defective performance of services has to inform UGAP through a webpage. UGAP monitors that and forwards the information to the supplier. The supplier has 48 hours to solve the problem otherwise he can be excluded from the next phases of the framework agreement.

Source: OECD (forthcoming), *Improving ISSSTE's Public Procurement for Better Results.*

Box 3.11. **A strategic sourcing and collaborative approach: Cleaning services in Croatia**

Cleaning is defined as the process of removing dirt, dust, organic matter and other stains from the floor, equipment and furniture in order to achieve an acceptable standard of cleanliness associated with the aesthetic appearance of space by using and combining different cleaning techniques. Cleaning services was a suitable category to be split by regions, and therefore for creating a framework agreement.

First, market research was conducted in order to gain knowledge on the specificities related to cleaning services.

A few big suppliers of cleaning services were contacted and their experiences were discussed. This was a mandatory step before starting the demand aggregation, as the procurement team needed to understand how to formulate tables for the demand aggregation, what data to ask for, etc.

The procurement team learned about the classification of space, the types of cleaning services, the percentage of labour in the price of service per square metre, the types of cleaning products used, etc. Information on the current contracts of the cleaning service suppliers was also very useful.

As understood during the initial market research step, the two major classifications of cleaning services are per type of space and per frequency of cleaning.

A call for tender was published, with the following details:

- Procurement procedure: Open public procurement procedure to conclude an FA with at least three economic operators for a period of three years.
- Lots: Division of procurement into 30 lots. The largest city, Zagreb, was split into several lots according to the locations of the ministries.
- A detailed list of locations and cleaning surface quantities for each lot and for each location was provided.
- Selection criteria:
  - a list of the bidder's services contracts executed over the past three years, indicating the amount and service
  - bidder's registration, taxes, criminal record
  - tender guarantee.
- Additional requirements: List of cleaning products:
  - self-declaration with the list of cleaning products that the supplier is going to use
  - the list becomes a part of the FA and can be checked accordingly.
- Price definition and adjustment:
  - The bid price shall include all costs and discounts without VAT, including wages, supplies (garbage bags), accessories, machinery and materials for cleaning.
  - The price does not include hygienic supplies – toilet paper, hand towels, liquid soap, etc.
  - Changes of the unit prices are related to a change in the minimum wage in Croatia.

Box 3.11. **A strategic sourcing and collaborative approach: Cleaning services in Croatia *(continued)***

In order to support the bidders in making better offers and due to the varying quality of surfaces and spaces, suppliers were allowed to visit each location prior to bidding. Visits were arranged with advance notice with the designated contact person for each location. Documentation was provided in advance of the specified times when the inspections could be performed, as well as the contact persons of the ministries.

Certain important questions were raised during the design and execution phases of the FA, including:

- How can it be verified whether the bidder executes the service according to the standards set in the agreement?
- What should be done if the service is not performed according to the standards?
- What standards should be introduced for the cleaning services?
- How should the minimum wage for the cleaning profession be defined and calculated?

The FA expired in August 2014. The procedure for setting up a new FA for the next period started well in advance of the expiration date. A revision of the initial FA took place in order to identify which items needed to be adjusted as a result of external changes as well as feedback on the performance of the FA. Some new conditions that tailored the new tender included:

- a government decision on outsourcing
- problems reported with call-offs for the 30 lots; there were many changes of facilities during the FA period.

Further to the internal revision of the initial FA, meetings with CAs and suppliers were held. These helped to rationalise the amount of hours for cleaning and decrease the number of lots from 30 to 20.

Source: OECD (forthcoming), *Manual on Framework Agreements for Greece.*

Expansion of goods in MAS contracts

In addition to expanding MAS contracts for services, the Shopping Mall Planning Division is responsible for identifying new products suitable for MAS contracting and dramatically expanding the number of items currently available through the Online Shopping Mall. This effort is currently focused on goods receiving social attention, and goods related to safety and security.

Recommendations for the Shopping Mall Planning Division

As with the expansion of MAS contracts for services, the use of a commodity management approach could benefit the efforts to expand the range of goods available in the Online Shopping Mall. As with complex services, there are some goods that are not easy to buy according to readily standardised qualities or commercial and test standards. In these cases, and with the expertise of the industrial specialists, processes for evaluating proposals during second stage competition according to comprehensive assessment may allow for the inclusion in MAS contracting of products that were otherwise excluded. The experience of the United States in establishing better centralised purchasing for printers is a relevant example (see Box 3.12). It illustrates the importance of identifying the true cost drivers when evaluating contracting approaches designed to lead to increased efficiency and cost savings. Printers are a relatively simple, commoditised good, but driving real savings in their use requires a much more detailed and sustained approach than simply establishing effective framework agreements for their purchase. Similarly, purchase of more complicated goods and services will often require a more in-depth understanding of the product or service, as well as ongoing activity to ensure that buyers' behaviours (for instance, in conducting second stage competition among MAS contract stakeholders) lead to efficient outcomes.

Box 3.12. **PrintWise in the United States**

A Federal Strategic Sourcing Initiative (FSSI) was begun in the United States to standardise purchasing and drive cost savings through consolidation. As a team of commodity experts was assembled, it quickly became clear that, while printers themselves are a relatively simple commodity, driving true cost savings with respect to government printing was a much more complicated issue. The United States Government Accountability Office reported that federal agencies spent an average of USD 440.4 million a year in unnecessary printing, with few agencies having established or enforced printing guidelines detailing when it was appropriate to print or refrain from printing. A focus on the devices themselves would ignore these cost drivers, as well as the lifecycle costs of toner, ink and maintenance.

To address these issues, the FSSI Print Management initiative was the first strategic sourcing solution to include a behavioural component. In addition to providing a framework agreement for the purchase of printers and toners, this initiative, dubbed PrintWise, also included a detailed change management campaign to improve printing practices across the US government.

The PrintWise change management initiative is built around "Seven Steps to Lowering Print Costs Within 90 Days":

1. Set your default to "duplex" (double-sided) printing.
2. Set your default to "black-and-white" or "grayscale" (rather than "colour") printing.
3. Set your default to "draft" quality (rather than "high" quality) printing.
4. Use one of the three approved toner-efficient fonts (Times New Roman, Garamond, and Century Gothic).
5. Improve your use of sleep mode for your printers.
6. Encourage the removal of personal printers.
7. Freeze purchases of personal printers.

These steps were supported by a PrintWise Campaign Toolkit, containing a guide for how to implement PrintWise at the agency level, a series of guiding principles for leading change implementation, resources for communications officials and a "message map," as well as graphical logos and posters, tent cards and stickers that could be used as visual elements in support of the change.

Source: General Services Administration (n.d.), "Printwise campaign toolkit", United States, https://strategicsourcing.gov/ printwise-campaign-toolkit (accessed 16 October 2015).

This is also an area where more comprehensive procurement data of the sort that will be available in the Public Procurement Data System will be very useful. As one of the criteria for establishing MAS contracts is sufficient cross-government demand, a clearer picture of that demand, incorporating all public buyers, can help inform the New Product Development Team as they look for additional products to include in MAS contracting.

Key findings and recommendations

PPS implementation of MAS contracting offers a number of examples of good practices, particularly in the areas of standardisation, efficiency and competition. By developing a uniform process that also allows for appropriate flexibility, many elements of the OECD Recommendation are addressed through implementation of MAS.

Element IV (ii) of the OECD Recommendation calls for the delivery of "clear and integrated tender documentation, standardised where possible and proportionate to the need." MAS contracting satisfies this element in a number of ways. The potential for vendors to apply for MAS contracts on a rolling timetable serves to "encourage broad participation from potential competitors." Standard processes for the establishment of and ordering from MAS contracts involves "providing clear guidance to inform buyers' expectations and binding information about evaluation and award criteria and their weights." The process of pre-qualification review helps to ensure that "the extent and complexity of information required in tender documentation and the time allotted for suppliers to respond is proportionate to the size and complexity of the procurement." This purpose is also served by the requirements for second stage competition, and the availability of a variety of assessment mechanisms for such competitions – simple needs can be satisfied with lowest price competitions, while goods to satisfy more complex needs are assessed according to more detailed criteria. MAS contracting also supports Element IV (iii) of the OECD Recommendation, encouraging competition both by providing an open-market environment for new vendors who would like to add their products and by explicitly requiring second stage competition in the case of large purchases.

MAS contracting also supports Element VII, "processes to drive efficiency throughout the public procurement cycle in satisfying the needs of the government and its citizens." The purpose of MAS contracting – to reduce duplication, inefficiency and waste by establishing framework agreements – is in line with Element VII (i), by streamlining the public procurement system and its institutional frameworks. By allowing dedicated PPS contracting officials to manage the work of establishing the MAS contracts, officials in other public-buying entities are freed to order with reduced burden and overlap, and to focus their own efforts on purchases with high priority within their organisations.

The implementation of MAS contracting also satisfies Element VII (ii), as a "sound technical process to satisfy customer needs efficiently." Identifying relevant targets for the award of MAS contracts and conducting the initial competition involves "developing appropriate technical specifications," and the decision to apply pre-qualification testing involves "identifying appropriate award criteria." PPS officials maintain the MAS contracts throughout their life, "ensuring adequate resources and expertise are available for contract management following the award of a contract." The establishment of centralised purchasing and framework agreements (such as MAS contracts) are explicit examples contained in Element VII (iii) of the OECD Recommendation. Further, this element calls for "application of such tools across sub-national levels of government, where appropriate," which is implemented through the availability to order from MAS contracts across the levels of government in Korea.

Given these good practices in implementing MAS contracting by PPS, the recommendations for improvement in this area focus largely on expansion of the system, rather than on necessary improvements.

Summary of recommendations

- Consider the necessity of the restriction on discounts during the second stage competition, and perhaps study whether 10% is the appropriate threshold.
- Consider implementation of broader commodity management efforts to allow for MAS contracts for complex services.
- Consider implementation of commodity management to allow for MAS contracts for non-standard goods.
- Consider workforce training and skills requirements necessary to support implementation of more complex MAS contracts for services and non-standard goods.
- Utilise whole-of-government data available from the Public Procurement Data System to develop a better understanding of demand in looking for additional products for MAS contracts.

References

General Services Administration (n.d.), "Printwise campaign toolkit", United States, https://strategicsourcing.gov/printwise-campaign-toolkit (accessed 16 October 2015).

Lyons, Grant (2013) Presentation made in Kosovo for the World Bank Workshop.

Magina, Paulo (2013), "The national public procurement system of Portugal", presentation made in Kuwait for the MENA-OECD Network on Public Procurement.

OECD (forthcoming), *Improving ISSSTE's Public Procurement for Better Results.*

OECD (forthcoming), *Manual on Framework Agreements for Greece.*

OECD (2015), "Recommendation of the Council on Public Procurement", www.oecd.org/corruption/recommendation-on-public-procurement.htm.

Chapter 4

Social integration: PPS implementation of secondary policy objectives

Korea utilises public procurement to support the furtherance of policy objectives through a broad and complex array of support mechanisms. These are primarily implemented by the Public Procurement Service (PPS) with support from other relevant ministries. This chapter presents an analysis of the use of public procurement to foster secondary policy objectives in Korea in three primary areas: support for particular types of enterprises, innovation and support for green public procurement.

While efficiency and cost effectiveness are among the primary objectives of public procurement, governments increasingly use this purchasing power as a policy lever to support various secondary objectives such as green growth, the development of small and medium-sized enterprises (SMEs), or innovation. The OECD has monitored these trends as part of its efforts to review country progress in implementing the 2008 OECD "Recommendation of the Council on Enhancing Integrity in Public Procurement", as well as in the development of public procurement data for the *OECD Governance at a Glance*.

The 2015 OECD "Recommendation of the Council on Public Procurement" (hereafter, the "OECD Recommendation") encourages a balanced approach to the inclusion of policy goals in public procurement. Recognising the delivery of goods and services necessary to accomplish government mission in a timely, economical and efficient manner as the primary procurement objective, the OECD Recommendation identifies secondary policy objectives as any of a variety of objectives pursued through public procurement, such as sustainable green growth, the development of small and medium-sized enterprises, innovation, standards for responsible business conduct or broader industrial policy objectives. The policy choice regarding whether to pursue secondary policy objectives in public procurement will vary by government and the needs of citizens, but the OECD Recommendation identifies steps that should be taken whenever such objectives are pursued (see Box 4.1).

Box 4.1. **OECD Recommendation on secondary policy objectives**

V. RECOMMENDS that Adherents recognise that any use of the public procurement system to pursue secondary policy objectives should be **balanced** against the primary procurement objective.

To this end, Adherents should:

i) **Evaluate the use of public procurement as one method of pursuing secondary policy objectives in accordance with clear national priorities**, balancing the potential benefits against the need to achieve value for money. Both the capacity of the procurement workforce to support secondary policy objectives and the burden associated with monitoring progress in promoting such objectives should be considered.

ii) **Develop an appropriate strategy for the integration of secondary policy objectives in public procurement systems.**For secondary policy objectives that will be supported by public procurement, appropriate planning, baseline analysis, risk assessment and target outcomes should be established as the basis for the development of action plans or guidelines for implementation.

iii) **Employ appropriate impact assessment methodology to measure the effectiveness of procurement in achieving secondary policy objectives.** The results of any use of the public procurement system to support secondary policy objectives should be measured according to appropriate milestones to provide policy makers with necessary information regarding the benefits and costs of such use. Effectiveness should be measured both at the level of individual procurements, and against policy objective target outcomes. Additionally, the aggregate effect of pursuing secondary policy objectives on the public procurement system should be periodically assessed to address potential objective overload.

Source: OECD (2015a), "Recommendation of the Council on Public Procurement", www.oecd.org/corruption/recommendation-on-public-procurement.htm.

The vast majority of OECD member countries use public procurement as a tool to implement policies or strategies to foster secondary policy objectives. In fact, 26 OECD member countries have developed strategies or policies to support green public procurement, SMEs and innovative goods and services. These strategies are predominantly developed at the central level (see Table 4.1).

Table 4.1. **Development of strategic public procurement by objective**

	Green public procurement	Support to SMEs	Support to innovative goods and services
Australia	●	●	●
Austria	●	○	●
Belgium	♦●	●	●
Canada	♦●	●	●
Chile	♦●	♦●	●
Denmark	●	●	●
Estonia	○	○	○
Finland	●	♦	♦
France	♦●	♦●	♦●
Germany	●	●	●
Greece	♦●	●	○
Hungary	♦	●	●
Ireland	●	●	●
Italy	♦	♦	♦
Japan	●	●	●
Korea	●	●	●
Luxembourg	♦●	♦●	♦
Mexico	●	●	●
New Zealand	♦●	♦●	♦●
Norway	◘	♦●	♦●
Poland	●	●	●
Portugal	●	♦	♦
Slovak Republic	○	○	○
Slovenia	♦●	●	●
Spain	♦●	♦●	♦●
Sweden	♦●	●	●
Switzerland	♦●	♦●	♦
United Kingdom	●	●	●
United States	●	●	♦●
Brazil	♦●	♦●	●
Colombia	♦	●	●
OECD29			
♦ A strategy / policy has been developed by some procuring entities	13	10	10
● A strategy/policy has been developed at a central level	24	23	20
◘ A strategy / policy has been rescinded	1	0	0
○ A strategy/policy has never been developed	2	3	3

Source: OECD (2015b), *Government at a Glance 2015*, OECD Publishing, Paris, http://dx.doi.org/10.1787/gov_glance-2015-en.

In sharp contrast, the number of OECD member countries that report measuring the results of their strategies or policies to promote environmental or socio-economic objectives is significantly lower and exhibits differences between the policy objectives. Among the 26 OECD member countries who have a strategy or policy developed at the central level or by procuring entities (line ministries), 18 (69%) measure the results of their strategy or policy to support green public procurement. There are 15 OECD member countries (58%) that measure the results of their strategy or policy to support SMEs. Only

9 OECD member countries (35%) measure the impact of their policy or strategy to foster innovative goods and services (see Figure 4.1).

Figure 4.1. **Measuring results of strategic public procurement's policies/strategies**

A. Support for green public procurement

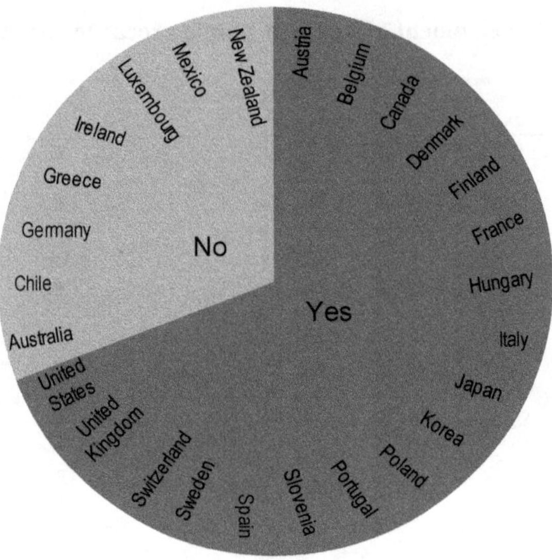

B. Support for SMEs

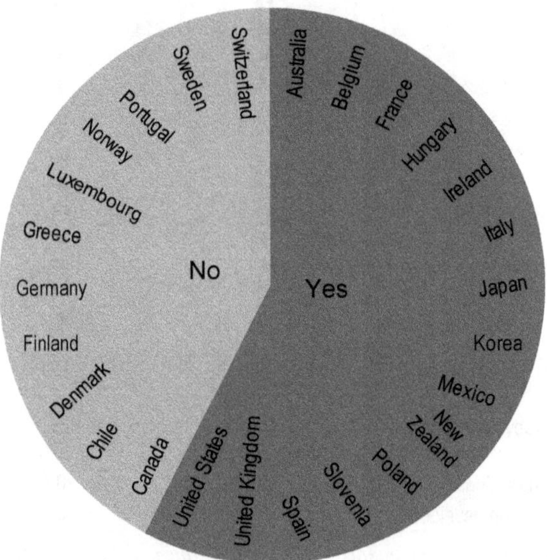

Figure 4.1. **Measuring results of strategic public procurement's policies/strategies** *(continued)*

C. Support for innovative goods and services

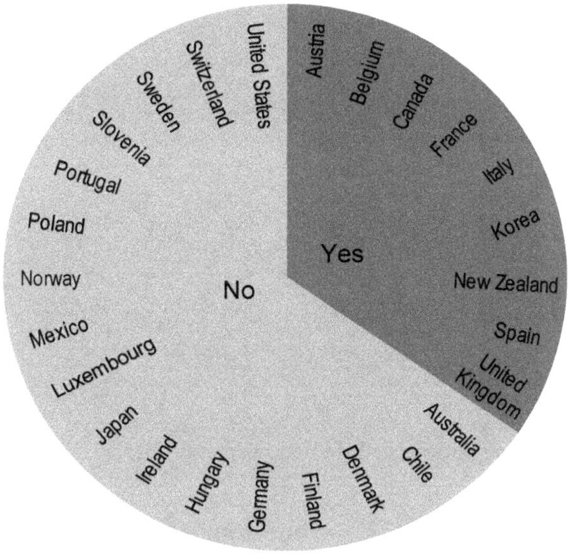

Source: OECD (2015b), *Government at a Glance 2015*, OECD Publishing, Paris, http://dx.doi.org/10.1787/gov_glance-2015-en.

PPS policies for supporting social enterprises

Public Procurement Service (PPS) implements the government's policies for increasing public purchases from a variety of types of entities, including small and medium-sized businesses, local businesses, women-owned businesses and other social enterprises.

Support for small and medium-sized enterprises

Support for SMEs in Korea is a strong priority, given the make-up of the economy. There are approximately 3.3 million SMEs in Korea, while there are only 2 900 large businesses: SMEs are 99.9% of businesses. This difference is reflected in the number of SMEs registered with PPS (see Table 4.2). Only 1.8 million employees work for large businesses, while SMEs employ 13 million, or 87.6% of the workforce. An estimated 47.7% of the value-added generated by the Korean economy is attributed to SMEs.

Table 4.2. **Registered Businesses in KONEPS**

		2009	2010	2011	2012	2013	2014
Total		262 411	261 314	291 245	323 003	353 021	384 994
Small and medium-sized businesses (including non-profit orgs.)	Subtotal	260 973	259 871	289 068	319 853	348 178	379 927
	General goods	106 864	105 432	119 694	134 932	149 417	166 766
	Foreign goods	5 205	5 069	5 417	5 675	5 985	6 212
	Public works	81 715	74 483	77 226	80 008	82 523	85 186
	Services	65 696	74 235	85 973	98 332	109 170	120 472
	Commodities	1 294	424	506	611	722	892
	Foreign firms	199	228	252	295	361	399
Large businesses	Subtotal	1 438	1 443	2 177	3 150	4 843	5 067
	General goods	586	581	886	1 271	1 886	2 000
	Foreign goods	67	58	70	107	151	148
	Public Works	308	312	456	632	945	974
	Services	441	464	732	1,105	1 845	1 923
	Commodities	9	1	6	8	16	22
	Foreign firms	27	27	27	27	0	0

Source: PPS response to OECD internal questionnaire, 2014 with updates in 2015.

The legal basis of support of SMEs comes from Article 4 of the Act on Facilitation of Purchase of Small and Medium Enterprise Manufactured Products and Support for Development of Their Markets, which requires the heads of public institutions to provide small and medium-sized businesses with increased opportunities to receive orders when they intend to make procurement contracts for goods, services and construction works. In the past, SMEs were defined by Article 3 of the Framework Act on Small and Medium Enterprises on the basis of either number of permanent employees, overall capital or sales volume. A recent change, which took effect on 1 January 2015, now defines SMEs solely in terms of sales volume (either annual or average). In addition to the criteria for being included as an SME, there are specific factors that can exclude an enterprise from SME status, including total assets exceeding USD 423.8 million. Finally, in addition to meeting the other criteria, a business must also be deemed independent in ownership and business operation (not a subsidiary of a large enterprise) with respect to the relevant laws and regulations.

Businesses must renew SME certification annually, and apply for certification by submitting corporate balance sheets to prove sales volume. Certification is conducted by the Small and Medium Business Administration (SMBA) according to the terms of Article 27 of the Small and Medium Business Framework Act.

Article 4 of the Enforcement Decree of the Act on Facilitation of Purchase of Small and Medium Enterprise-Manufactured Products and Support for Development of their Markets sets an annual purchasing goal for SME-manufactured products of 50% or more of total purchasing value.

For goods and services procurement, SMEs are supported through a broad range of programmes. An SME set-aside programme is run in co-operation with the Small and Medium Business Administration (SMBA). Under this programme, SMBA designates specific products for SMEs, and currently there are 207 products with this designation. For these products designated as competitive products, only SMEs that directly manufacture such products are invited to participate in competitive tenders. Eligibility to participate is managed through a Public E-procurement Information Network, available at www.smpp.go.kr and maintained by SMBA. Direct contracting is allowed for small-sum contracts (below USD 42 400). In order to prevent excessive competition resulting in unsustainably low prices, discounts below 88% of the established reference price are not allowed (see Chapter 3 for more information on the establishment of reference prices).

In addition to the set-aside programme, large businesses are restricted from participation in tenders for general goods below the World Trade Organization Agreement on Government Procurement (WTO GPA) threshold. There are also SME-related requirements during the second stage competition related to Multiple Award Schedule (MAS) framework agreements, for appropriate products. The award period for MAS contracts was recently doubled to two years, in most categories, as a means of reducing the burden on SMEs of applying for these contracts on an annual basis.

On the basis of these programmes, SMEs captured a substantial share of over 50% of contracts conducted by competition in 2013, a significant increase from the 30% share of 2009, as shown in Table 4.3.

Table 4.3. **Contract performance by competition among SMEs**

In USD billions

Categories	2009	2010	2011	2012	2013	2014
Competition contracting (A)	11.4	11.3	12.0	13.4	14.7	11.8
Competition among SMEs (B)	3.5	4.3	5.7	6.9	7.7	6.3
Percentage	30.5%	38.2%	47.8%	51.5%	52.1%	53.7%

Source: PPS response to OECD internal questionnaire, 2014 with updates in 2015.

SMEs can also benefit from a variety of special designations that are offered by SMBA, PPS and line ministries. Designation as an outstanding SME (for example, through certification for excellent technology or performance, or through designation as an innovative SME by SMBA) provides additional points in contract fulfilment capability tests, allowing such SMEs a competitive advantage. Designation as a supplier of an Excellent Government Supply Product allows for direct contracting, which can increase SME market share. The Excellent Government Supply Joint Brands designation allows direct contracting in a way that supports technology sharing, transfer and joint production among SMEs. These and other certification mechanisms will be examined in more detail below.

For construction works, the Korean Government assigns some projects into multi-use lists that are divided into seven classes according to the size of the work. For works of second class and below (Class 1 is the largest), only small and medium-sized construction companies are allowed to participate in tenders (a breakdown of construction works by class is presented in Table 4.4). These classes include works below USD 127 million for civil engineering works, and works below USD 93.2 million for architectural works. Many of the 207 designated products set aside for SMEs are construction materials. Korea has also recently implemented a programme to better support subcontractors by protecting their rights to timely payments and preventing "dual contracts" that forced subcontractors to perform according to less favourable terms following award of the government contract. This system, the Subcontract Management System for Government Contracts (SMSGC) is demonstrating impressive results in its initial implementation. More detail on SMSGC is presented in Chapter 2.

Table 4.4. **Construction works contracts**

In USD billions

		2009	2010	2011	2012	2013	2014
New construction works contracts total		22.3	12.6	9.4	8.2	9.1	7.3
Volume of contracts where multi-use list applies	Class 1	1.9	0.7	0.8	1.4	0.6	0.3
	Class 2 and below	3.3	2.0	1.3	1.6	1.5	1.8
	Subtotal	5.2	2.7	201	3.0	2.1	2.0
Percentage (Total/Class 2 and below)		14.9%	15.9%	13.4%	19.4%	17.0%	28.1%

Source: PPS response to OECD internal questionnaire, 2014 with updates in 2015.

PPS also provides special financial support to SMEs involved in public contracting. SMEs are entitled to an upfront payment of up to 70% of the value of a government contract (see Table 4.5). For some contracts for goods, including orders against unit-price contracts, lump sum contracts for goods valued up to USD 423 800, or at the request of the end user for other goods contracts, the business is entitled to instant payment upon presentation of the invoice. In these cases, payment is made from the PPS special account and then reimbursed by the end user, as discussed in Chapter 2. Though central government entities are entitled to a payment period of up to five days, instant payment allows SMEs to receive payment within as little as four working hours.

Table 4.5. **Upfront payment**

In USD millions

	2009	2010	2011	2012	2013	2014
Total upfront payment	409.4	372.4	301.0	418.9	488.7	479.0
Upfront payment to SMEs	251.6	348.4	291.4	389.1	447.1	443.8
Percentage	61.4%	93.6%	96.8%	92.9%	91.5%	92.7%

Source: PPS response to OECD internal questionnaire, 2014 with updates in 2015.

Further liquidity support for SMEs in public procurement comes from a network loan programme. Under this programme, 15 commercial banks have partnered with PPS to offer terms that allow SMEs to obtain loans for up to 80% of the contract amount solely based on the contract with PPS, without any lien. This is a valuable means of support for SMEs without the financial standing to otherwise finance performance of public procurement contracts, and it has expanded substantially in recent years, reaching over 11 000 loans and nearly USD 400 million (see Table 4.6). Six institutions - including KIBO (Korea Technical Finance Corporation), Korea Federation of SMEs, Industrial Bank of Korea, Sinhan Bank, Hana Bank and Woori Bank – provide even more comprehensive support for SMEs in the form of warranties, loans and enterprise consulting. As of 31 December 2014, 1 223 warranties, loans and consultations were provided under this programme, for a total amount of USD 571 million.

Table 4.6. **Network loans made to SMEs**

	2009	2010	2011	2012	2013	2014
Number of loans	933	4 754	7 541	10 048	11 472	11 419
Amount (in USD millions)	50.8	147.7	250.6	341.0	398.6	378.6

Source: PPS response to OECD internal questionnaire, 2014 with updates in 2015.

Data regarding PPS contract awards to SMEs are contained in Table 4.7, and are further broken down by category in Tables 4.8 and 4.9. In general, SMEs account for two-thirds of total contracting value awarded by PPS. Table 4.10 shows that the PPS proportion of SME contracting relative to total contracting in Korea is around one-third.

Table 4.7. **Total contract awards to SMEs**

In USD billions

	2009	2010	2011	2012	2013	2014
Total contract awards	36.2	32.0	28.2	29.0	32.1	28.3
Awards to SMEs	19.4	19.1	18.5	19.0	21.3	20.4
Percentage of awards to SMEs	53.6%	59.8%	65.7%	65.3%	66.4%	71.9%

Source: PPS response to OECD internal questionnaire, 2014 with updates in 2015.

Table 4.8. **Contract awards to SMEs for goods and services**

In USD billions

		2009	2010	2011	2012	2013	2014
Total contract awards for goods and services		16.0	14.7	15.2	16.9	19.0	19.1
Awards to SMEs[1]	Goods	10.0	9.7	10.5	11.4	12.8	12.7
	Services	1.3	1.4	1.3	1.5	2.0	2.1
	Total	11.3	11.1	11.8	13.0	14.9	14.8
Percentage of awards to SMEs		70.9%	75.2%	77.6%	76.6%	78.1%	77.4%

1. Awards to social organisations, cooperatives, and social enterprises that meet the SME criteria are included in the figures as of 1 July 2013.

Source: PPS response to OECD internal questionnaire, 2014 with updates in 2015.

Table 4.9. **Contract awards to SMEs for construction works**

In USD billions

		2009	2010	2011	2012	2013	2014
Total contract awards for construction works		20.3	17.3	13.0	12.2	13.1	9.2
Awards to SMEs	Construction	8.1	8.0	6.6	5.9	6.2	5.4
	Technical consultancy services[1]	0*	0.2	0.2	0.1	0.2	0.2
	Total	8.1	8.1	6.7	6.0	6.4	5.6
Percentage of awards to SMEs		39.9%	46.7%	51.8%	49.7%	49.3%	60.5%

1. Until the end of 2009, technical consultancy services had been categorised under goods and services.

Source: PPS response to OECD internal questionnaire, 2014 with updates in 2015.

Table 4.10. **PPS' share in total public procurement contract awards to SMEs**

In USD billions

	2009	2010	2011	2012	2013
Total public procurement contract awards to SMEs[1]	67.6	56.8	57.4	61.0	66.8
PPS's contract awards to SMEs*	19.4	19.1	18.5	19.0	21.3
Percentage	28.7%	33.7%	32.3%	31.1%	31.9%

1. Figure includes PPS's contract awards to SMEs for general goods and services and construction works. Awards for foreign procurement and commodity stockpiling/release are not included in this figure.

Source: PPS response to OECD internal questionnaire, 2014 with updates in 2015.

Recommendations for improvement of SME support

During the fact-finding mission, it was identified that the public procurement system in Korea can tend to seem overly focused on SMEs, to the exclusion of large suppliers. While much of this focus is intentional, additional steps could mitigate this concern to some extent. PPS should consider evaluating tenders from large suppliers on the basis of support for SMEs provided through subcontracting opportunities. While some subcontracting is set aside for SMEs through various other programmes, there is no systematic method for encouraging large enterprises to subcontract with SMEs. Such programmes in other countries serve to further increase procurement opportunities for SMEs while also demonstrating the value of large enterprises for high-value procurements (see the example from the United States in Box 4.2).

Box 4.2. **Small business subcontracting in the United States**

As an additional method of encouraging participation by small businesses in federal contracting opportunities, the United States has implemented a mandatory Small Business Subcontracting Program. For all contracts that exceed the simplified acquisition threshold (USD 150 000), contractors are expected to provide the maximum practicable opportunity to participate in contract performance to small business, veteran-owned small business, services-disabled veteran-owned small business, Historically Underutilized Business Zone (HUBZone) small business, small disadvantaged business, and women-owned small business concerns. For contracts or contract modifications expected to exceed USD 650 000 (including options) that contain subcontracting opportunities, the supplier selected for award is required to submit a detailed subcontracting plan. Failure to submit a subcontracting plan renders the supplier ineligible for award, and any contractor or subcontractor that fails to comply in good faith with the requirements of the subcontracting plan is considered in material breach of its contract. The requirement for a subcontracting plan does not apply when the selected supplier is itself a small business, to personal services contracts, or to contracts performed entirely outside of the United States (FAR 19.702).

Each subcontracting plan must include:

1. separate percentage goals for small business, veteran-owned small business, service-disabled veteran owned small business, HUBZone small business, small disadvantaged business and women-owned small business concerns as subcontractors

Box 4.2. **Small business subcontracting in the United States** *(continued)*

2. a statement of the total dollars planned to be subcontracted and the total dollars planned to be subcontracted to the categories of concerns identified in (1)
3. a description of the principal types of supplies and services to be subcontracted, including identification of the types to be subcontracted to the relevant concerns
4. a description of the method used to develop the subcontracting goals
5. a description of the method used to identify potential sources for solicitation purposes
6. a statement as to whether indirect cost considerations were included in the establishment of goals and estimated share of subcontracts
7. the name of an individual who will administer the subcontracting program, and a description of the duties of the individual;
8. a description of the efforts the offeror will make to ensure that relevant suppliers have an equitable opportunity to compete for the subcontracts
9. assurances that the offeror will include the clause that mandates the Small Business Subcontracting Program in all subcontracts that offer further subcontracting opportunities and require any such subcontracts that exceed USD 650 000 to include their own small business subcontracting plan
10. assurances that the offeror will co-operate in any surveys, studies and reporting requirements necessary
11. a description of the types of records that will be maintained concerning procedures adopted to comply with the requirements and goals in the plan.

Rather than establishing a subcontracting plan for each contract action, contractors may establish a master plan on a plant- or division-wide basis that contains all of the elements necessary except specific goals. For individual contracts, the master plan is then incorporated into the individual subcontracting plan along with the goals for that contract. Such plans are effective for three years after approval, but it remains a contractor's responsibility to maintain and update the master plan. Any changes to the master plan must be approved by the contracting officer (FAR 19.704).

In addition to the compliance requirements imposed by the subcontracting plan, the contracting officer may encourage the development of increased subcontracting opportunities in negotiated acquisition by providing monetary incentives in the form of payments based on actual subcontracting achievement or award-fee contracting. Such incentives are only appropriate when the contracting officer ensures that the goals are realistic and that any such incentives are commensurate with efforts the contractor would not have otherwise expended to achieve them (FAR 19.705).

Source: United States Federal Acquisition Regulation 48 CFR 19.7, www.acquisition.gov/sites/default/files/current/far/html/Subpart%2019_7.html#wp1088741.

Support for local businesses

Both the State Contracts Act and the Local Government Contract Act specify requirements to limit competition to local bidders, below certain thresholds (see Table 4.11).

Table 4.11. **Competition restricted to local bidders**

	Legal basis and application thresholds	
	Central government entities	Local government entities
Legal provisions	Enforcement Decree of the State Contract Act Article 21 Paragraph 1-6, Enforcement Regulations of the State Contract Act Article 24 Paragraph 2	Enforcement Decree of the Local Government Contract Act Article 1 Paragraph 6, Enforcement Regulations of the Local Government Contract Act Article 24 Paragraph 2
Composite works	Below USD 7 million	Below USD 8.5 million
Specialty works,	Below USD 600 000	Below USD 600 000 (For administrative city projects, below USD 850 000)
Other works	Below USD 600 000	Below USD 425 000
Goods (manufacture or supply), services	Below USD 178 000	Below USD 280 000 (Provincial govts. and metropolitan city govts.) Below USD 425 000 (Municipality govts.)

Source: PPS response to OECD internal questionnaire, 2014 with updates in 2015.

For goods and services, details regarding the amount of contracting conducted through restricted competition below the established thresholds is presented in Table 4.12, which indicates a low use of this prerogative.

Table 4.12. **Goods and services contracting through restricted competition**

In USD millions

	2009	2010	2011	2012	2013	2014
Total contract awards for goods and services	15 965.4	14 706.0	15 204.6	16 899.1	19 039.3	19 105.2
Contract awards through restricted competition among local businesses	110.3	106.6	110.5	107.6	49.1	1.4
Percentage	0.7%	0.7%	0.7%	0.6%	0.3%	0.0%

Source: PPS response to OECD internal questionnaire, 2014 with updates in 2015.

In addition to these requirements for locality-based contracting of overall projects, additional provisions exist that require obligatory subcontracting with local businesses. A mandatory joint local subcontract system must be applied for central government construction works below USD 7 million and public institution construction works below USD 20.8 million. All local government construction work should apply this mandatory joint local subcontract system, but an exception applies to local government construction works that exceed USD 20.8 million that were open to international tender and include a foreign construction firm as one of the contract winners.

Information regarding purchases through restricted competition and obligatory subcontracting is presented in Table 4.13, demonstrating that more than 50% of construction contracts are subject to such restrictions. Additional preference for local business products applies to categories such as ready-mixed concrete, asphalt-concrete and cement products for suppliers located in the region where the work takes place, and direct contracting is allowed for goods produced by disabled veterans' businesses and businesses located in industrial complexes in rural areas. PPS is also working to increase MAS contracts with local businesses.

Table 4.13. **Construction Contracting Through Restricted Competition and Obligatory Subcontracting**

In USD billions

	2009	2010	2011	2012	2013	2014
New construction works contracts total	22.3	12.6	9.4	8.2	9.1	7.3
Contract awards through restricted competition among local businesses	2.0	1.8	1.6	1.4	1.6	1.4
Obligatory subcontracts to local businesses	7.2	4.5	2.2	3.1	3.5	3.3
Subtotal	9.2	6.3	3.7	4.6	5.2	4.7
Percentage (Subtotal/Total)	41.0%	50.2%	39.5%	55.7%	57.1%	64.7%

Source: PPS response to OECD internal questionnaire, 2014 with updates in 2015.

Overall data regarding PPS contract awards to local businesses are contained in Table 4.14 and is further broken down by category in Tables 4.15 and 4.16.

Table 4.14. **PPS total contract awards to local business**

In USD billions

	2009	2010	2011	2012	2013	2014
Total contract awards	36.2	32.0	28.2	29.0	32.1	28.3
Awards to local businesses	22.4	20.0	18.9	19.3	21.9	19.8
Percentage of awards to local businesses	62.0%	62.6%	66.8%	66.4%	68.2%	70.0%

Source: PPS response to OECD internal questionnaire, 2014 with updates in 2015.

Table 4.15. **PPS contract awards to local businesses for goods and services**

In USD billions

		2009	2010	2011	2012	2013	2014
Total contract awards for goods and services		16.0	14.7	15.2	16.9	19.0	19.1
Awards to local businesses	Goods	9.8	8.8	9.3	10.6	12.2	11.9
	Services	0.8	0.7	0.7	0.8	1.0	1.0
	Total	10.6	9.6	10.0	11.4	13.1	12.9
Percentage of awards to local businesses		66.5%	65.0%	65.6%	67.5%	68.8%	67.4%

Source: PPS response to OECD internal questionnaire, 2014 with updates in 2015.

Table 4.16. **PPS contract awards to local businesses for construction works**

In USD billions

		2009	2010	2011	2012	2013	2014
Total contract awards for construction works		20.3	17.3	13.0	12.2	13.1	9.2
Awards to local businesses	Construction	11.8	10.4	8.8	7.8	8.7	6.8
	Technical consultancy services	0	0.1	0.1	0.1	0.1	0.1
	Total	11.8	10.5	8.9	7.9	8.8	7.0
Percentage of awards to local businesses		58.4%	60.7%	68.2%	64.9%	67.3%	75.3%

Source: PPS response to OECD internal questionnaire, 2014 with updates in 2015.

Support for women-owned businesses

Article 4 of the Act on Support for Female-owned Businesses instructs, "the head of a public entity shall promote the purchase of goods manufactured and supplied by women-owned small and medium businesses." Women-owned businesses are defined according to three criteria: *1)* the business is owned or managed by a woman; *2)* a woman is registered as the executive representing the business; or *3)* the business registration was made by a woman pursuant to the Income Tax Act or the Value-added Tax Act. Article 7 of the Enforcement Decree of Act on Support for Female-owned Businesses sets target goals for procurement from women-owned business at 5% or more of total purchasing value of goods and services, and 3% or more of total purchasing value of construction works.

This instruction is implemented through two provisions that allow direct contracting with women-owned businesses. With respect to goods and services procurement, Article 90 of the PPS Regulation of Domestic Procurement Process indicates, "Where the estimated price of a contract is below KRW 20 million and there is no supplier recommended by the end-user entity, the contractor shall be decided through price quotation and negotiation with a women-owned business or a disabled persons' business recommended by the relevant associations." For such contracts, PPS directly awards to a woman-owned business recommended by the Review Committee for Recommendations for Small Direct Contracts, which is composed of four women's associations. For goods tenders, women-owned businesses and businesses with high employment of women or gender equality are given additional points in the contract fulfilment capability test, as indicated in Table 4.17.

Table 4.17. **Women-owned business priority in the capability test**

Categories	Additional points (out of 100 scale)
Women-owned enterprises	For women-owned businesses that have existed for three years or longer: Additional 0.5 point For women-owned businesses that have existed for less than three years: Additional 0.25 point
Businesses with high employment of women	For businesses with 10% or higher employment of women (provided that the number of women employees exceeds ten): Additional 1.25 points For businesses with 5~10% employment of women (provided that the number of women employees exceeds five): Additional 0.75 point
Gender equality businesses	"Gender Equality Business" certified by the Ministry of Employment and Labour: Additional 1.0 point

Source: PPS response to OECD internal questionnaire, 2014 with updates in 2015.

Women-owned businesses are also given additional points when selecting Excellent Government Supply Products, with three additional points being awarded for women-owned venture companies, "INNO-BIZ" companies or Innovative SMEs, and two points for products manufactured by women-owned businesses outside these categories.

Article 19 of the PPS Regulation on Construction Works Contracting Process adds, "Where the estimated price of the work is below the designated threshold and there is no supplier recommended by the end-user entity, the head of responsible regional PPS office may select a woman-owned business and negotiate for direct contracting." Details of the application of this provision appear in Table 4.18.

Table 4.18. **Construction contracting with women-owned businesses**

Threshold			Contracting method
General work	Specialty work	Electricity, ICT, Firefighting work	
Below USD 17 000	Below USD 17 000	Below USD 17 000	Direct contracting with local SMEs, or quotation competition among local women-owned businesses
USD 17 000 ~ USD 42 500	USD 17 000 ~ USD 42 500	USD 17 000 ~ USD 42 500	Direct contracting with local SMEs (including women-owned or handicapped suppliers), or quotation competition among local women-owned businesses
USD 42 500 ~ USD 85 000	-	-	Quotation competition among local women-owned businesses
USD 85 000 ~ USD 170 000	USD 42 500 ~ USD 85 000	USD 42 500 ~ USD 68 000	Quotation competition among local SMEs

Source: PPS response to OECD internal questionnaire, 2014 with updates in 2015.

Implementation of these programmes has led to a steady increase in the number and proportion of women-owned businesses registered with PPS, almost reaching 20% in 2013, as demonstrated in Table 4.19.

Table 4.19. **Number of registered women-owned businesses**

	2009	2010	2011	2012	2013	2014
Registered businesses total	262 411	261 314	291 245	323 003	350 338	384 994
Women-owned businesses	41 034	43 542	49 525	56 535	63 666	71 848
Percentage	15.6%	16.7%	17.0%	17.5%	18.2%	18.7%

Source: PPS response to OECD internal questionnaire, 2014 with updates in 2015.

Statistics regarding PPS contract awards to women-owned businesses, currently around 6% of the total, is contained in Table 4.20, and is further broken down by category in Tables 4.21 and 4.22, showing a higher than average awarding percentage for goods and services and below average awarding for construction works, which is generally aligned with the nature of the delivery. Table 4.23 shows the PPS proportion of contracting with women-owned businesses relative to total contracting in Korea, over 50% of the total in 2013, signalling a relevant capacity of PPS to develop this specific programme.

Table 4.20. **PPS contract awards to women-owned businesses**

In USD billions

	2009	2010	2011	2012	2013	2014
Total contract awards	36.2	32.0	28.2	29.0	32.1	28.3
Awards to women-owned businesses	1.4	1.4	1.5	1.7	2.0	2.1
Percentage of awards to women-owned businesses	3.9%	4.4%	5.4%	5.9%	6.3%	7.5%

Source: PPS response to OECD internal questionnaire, 2014 with updates in 2015.

Table 4.21. **PPS contract awards to women-owned businesses for goods and services**

In USD billions

		2009	2010	2011	2012	2013	2014
Total contract awards for goods and services		16.0	14.7	15.2	16.9	19.0	19.1
Awards to women-owned businesses	Goods	0.8	0.7	0.8	1.0	1.2	1.3
	Services	0.2	0.2	0.2	0.2	0.3	0.3
	Total	0.9	0.9	1.0	1.2	1.5	1.6
Percentage of awards to women-owned businesses		5.8%	6.0%	6.8%	7.1%	7.6%	8.5%

Source: PPS response to OECD internal questionnaire, 2014 with updates in 2015.

Table 4.22. **PPS contract awards to women-owned businesses for construction works**

In USD millions

		2009	2010	2011	2012	2013	2014
Total contract awards for construction works (A)		20 257.8	1 301.2	13 016.1	12 150.4	13 081.1	9 238.8
Awards to women-owned businesses (B)	Construction	489.9	525.8	489.4	507.0	569.6	507.1
	Technical consultancy services	0	6.6	7.0	8.4	1.2	5.3
	Total	589.9	532.4	496.4	515.4	570.8	512.4
Percentage of awards to women-owned businesses (B/A)		2.4%	3.1%	3.8%	4.2%	4.4%	5.5%

Source: PPS response to OECD internal questionnaire, 2014 with updates in 2015.

Table 4.23. **PPS' share in total public procurement to women-owned businesses**

In USD billions

	2009	2010	2011	2012	2013
Total public procurement contract awards to women-owned businesses	2.58	2.0	2.2	2.9	3.8
PPS contract awards to women-owned businesses[1]	1.4	1.4	1.5	1.7	2.0
Percentage	54.7%	71.1%	69.5%	59.5%	53.2%

1. Figure includes PPS's contract awards to women-owned businesses for general goods and services, and construction works. Awards for foreign procurement and commodity stockpiling/release are not included in the figure.

Source: PPS response to OECD internal questionnaire, 2014 with updates in 2015.

Support for other social objectives

In addition to the programmes for supporting SMEs, local businesses and women-owned businesses, PPS also implements programmes to support other social objectives, such as veteran and welfare organisations, goods and services provided by persons with severe disabilities, businesses that produce traditional Korean craftwork and social enterprises.

For veteran and welfare organisations, PPS allocates certain goods to be contracted with these organisations through single-source (direct) contracting; these veteran and welfare organisations are defined in the State Contracts Act. Products manufactured by entitled organisations include switchboards, closed-circuit TV products, stage equipment, road signs, broadcasting equipment, lighting towers, landscape lighting and shoe cases, among others. PPS uses an apportionment scheme when purchasing products from entitled organisations, setting aside up to 20% of PPS' total purchase volume of each product. As the purpose of the policy is to support various disadvantaged groups, a controlled distribution of purchase orders is established to allow business to go to each entitled organisation. PPS conducts an annual Purchase Review Committee Meeting to establish the apportionment scheme according to which each organisation will receive orders.

Since the establishment of this programme in 1996, the volume of contracting with such organisations has increased dramatically, though it has reduced slightly in recent years (see Table 4.24).

Table 4.24. **Volume of single source contracting with veteran and welfare organisations**

In USD millions

	2009	2010	2011	2012	2013	2014
Total value of domestic procurement	15 965.4	14 706.0	15 204.6	16 899.1	19 039.3	19 105.2
Single source contracting with veteran and welfare organisations	177.3	159.4	135.5	117.9	153.1	165.5
Percentage	1.3%	1.1%	0.9%	0.7%	0.8%	0.9%

Source: PPS response to OECD internal questionnaire, 2014 with updates in 2015.

Goods and services provided by suppliers that hire persons with disabilities are provided preferential purchasing in order to create more job opportunities for such individuals. Overseen by the Ministry of Health and Welfare with input from the Korea Disabled People's Development Institute and the Korea Vocational Rehabilitation Association for the Disabled, this programme functions through the designation of categories such as office supplies, toilet paper, toothbrushes, gloves, furniture, paper cups, banners, books and printing. Within these categories, suppliers are identified; 404 suppliers were approved as of February 2015. Central government entities, local government entities and other public organisations such as educational institutes are required to submit an annual purchasing plan, the previous year's plan and a purchasing goal to the Minister of Health and Welfare, with a mandatory purchasing rate of more than 1% of the total purchasing value of each end user set by Article 10 of the

Enforcement Decree of Special Act on the Preferential Purchase of Products Manufactured by Persons with Severe Disabilities.

Since 1998, upon administrative order from the President and Prime Minister, PPS has undertaken to nurture Korean culture through the promotion of traditional craftwork. This programme was selected as one of 100 national projects to promote traditional craftwork for use by public organisations, as souvenirs and for event supplies in September of 1999. Since 2006, the Association of Government Procurement Cultural Goods has conducted the task of reviewing the selection of procurement goods subject to this programme. At any time of year, a manufacturer can register a traditional craftwork product. A committee composed of approximately ten experts recommended by PPS and the Cultural Heritage Administration then reviews these registrations. For goods designated as traditional craftwork, a single-source unit-price contract is conducted by PPS and supplied for use of other organisations through the KONEPS Online Shopping Mall. Such goods are also on display for purchase in an exhibit hall at the PPS headquarters in Daejeon City. Data regarding the value of traditional craftwork is provided in Table 4.25.

Table 4.25. **Performance of traditional craftwork**

In USD millions

	2009	2010	2011	2012	2013	2014
Total value supplied	1.8	0.8	1.0	1.9	1.8	2.2

Source: PPS response to OECD internal questionnaire, 2014 with updates in 2015.

Article 12 of the Social Enterprises Promotion Act requires the head of a public entity to promote the purchase of goods and services produced by social enterprises. Social enterprises are defined rather broadly, as businesses pursuing social goals such as providing services or job opportunities for socially disadvantaged groups, or contributing to local communities for raising the communities' standard of living. As of December 2014 there are 669 social enterprises registered with PPS. Support for these enterprises includes business consultancy for start-up social enterprises to broaden their public procurement market opportunities. Additionally, the KONEPS Online Shopping Mall contains a separate section for products from social enterprises, to raise their visibility in the public procurement market. PPS contract awards to social enterprises grew from USD 10.5 million in 2012 to USD 29.8 million in 2013 and USD 65.1 million in 2014.

Certification programmes and innovation

In addition to the programmes outlined above, there are a number of categories within the Korean public procurement system that allow for preferential purchasing of products with new technology. Products manufactured by newly developed technology are evaluated and awarded a New Excellent Product (NEP) certification, which allows preferential purchasing. In product categories where NEP products exist, central government agencies, local government entities and other public organisations are mandated to purchase more than 20% of their total volume within that category from NEP products. For such products, single-source contracting is allowed in accordance with Articles 26 Paragraph 1-3 of the Enforcement Decree of the Act on Contracts to Which the State is a Party.

In order to increase public purchase of new technology products developed by SMEs, SMBA designates newly developed technology products for priority purchase according to Article 14 of the Act on Facilitation of Purchase of Small and Medium Enterprises - Manufactured Products and Support for Development of their Markets, and Article 13 of its Enforcement Decree. Within this broad category of newly developed technology products, there is a complex collection of additional certifications, summarised in Box 4.3. Central government agencies and public organisations are mandated to purchase at least 10% of their purchases from SMEs from among SME-manufactured goods with new technology. To achieve this mandate, single-source contracting or selective competitive contracting is allowed in accordance with the Enforcement Decree of the Act on Contracts to Which the State is a Party.

Box 4.3. **Types of newly developed technology products**

1. Excellent Performance Certification (EPC): Certification given to new technology products developed by an SME.

2. Excellent Government Supply Products: Products excelling in performance, technology or quality. PPS designates products in this category, which allows direct contracting with any public entity.

3. New Excellent Product (NEP): Certification for new products using a technology that is newly developed in Korea, or that brings innovative improvements over existing ones.

4. Good Software Certification (GS): Certification for high quality software developed in Korea.

5. Eight other categories designated by SMBA:

   a. New Excellent Technology certified products
   b. Products developed from purchase-conditioned R&D (research and development) programme: developed under the scheme that the government subsidises R&D for product development with a view to purchasing the outcome product
   c. Green label products
   d. Products on Excellent Government Supply Joint Brand Programme
   e. Products from convergence and fusion technology development projects
   f. Products designated by Ministry of Trade, Industry and Energy as "industry fusion" products
   g. Select products from joint R&D projects between public entities and SMEs
   h. Products jointly developed on "technology development for shared outcome" projects, through collaboration among large enterprises and SMEs

These certification programmes represent a detailed and advanced approach to encouraging innovation through public procurement. As each certificate has a limited time before expiring, and the innovation that led to certification as new technology is not sufficient to obtain the next certificate, there is a constant pressure to provide new features, updated functionality and pioneering development to products proposed for government procurement. For suppliers, the focus is not so much on the goals set for government procurement from these categories, but on the competitive advantage that results from obtaining the certifications. During the fact-finding mission, suppliers identified the value of certifications as a distinguishing characteristic during MAS second stage competition and additional points on evaluation criteria as primary reasons for pursuing certifications. The fact that certification as an Excellent Government Supply Product allows direct contracting with any public entity for purchases is a substantial incentive to achieve this certification, though such purchase requests must be monitored to ensure that the product is purchased in accordance with relevant laws and regulations.

Despite these benefits, there are concerns that the programmes might not operate as efficiently or effectively as desired. During the fact-finding mission, the peers identified some concern among suppliers about the number of various certificates and the complexity of the system. Additionally, concern was expressed regarding the effectiveness of the certification programmes in truly identifying outstanding products: one supplier indicated that in categories where dozens of products all carry the Excellent Government Supply Product rating, despite sharp differences in quality and performance, the certificate is not as effective as it could be in identifying products truly worthy of support.

In addition to these concerns, there is also a substantial investment of time and resources that must be made to obtain these certifications, especially the Excellent Government Product Certification. One interview subject indicated that the total process will take between ten months and a year, for a certification that will last three years but can be extended up to three years based on meeting additional criteria (such as exporting a certain proportion of sales volume). This time is necessary because achieving the Excellent Government Product Certification requires many other certificates as a prerequisite, including a patent (which must be less than five years old) and achievement of an Excellent Performance Certificate from SMBA. The designation as an Excellent Government Product itself takes three months, and is processed four times per year by quarter, so timing the process correctly is important. Once designated, establishing the contract can take another two months. The need to obtain certifications of various sorts, including for environmental characteristics, was identified by another interview participant as an increased burden that applies to public procurement.

Recommendations for improvement of the certification processes

The fact-finding mission demonstrated that, despite the burden, suppliers were strongly motivated to pursue the certification because the benefits derived from the ability to receive direct awards was much more substantial than participation in framework agreements, generally. While this indicates that the certifications are working as an incentive, it is not clear that the current structure provides the most effective means of driving efficiency in public procurement. PPS, working with SMBA and other stakeholders including the Federation of SMEs, should evaluate the current structure of certificates. This evaluation should include means of simplifying the certification structure, as well as means of better promoting value through a meaningful comparison of new innovations.

As in many OECD countries, there is also a lack of established metrics to evaluate the effectiveness of these programmes, relative to their costs. While measuring the economic benefits to the companies that achieve the certificates as compared with their standing if they had not achieved the certificate is difficult, efforts should be made to balance these potential benefits against the cost of achieving certification. One additional concern is the fact that achievement of the pinnacle certificate, the Excellent Government Product

Certification, yields a limitation of competition through the ability to offer direct awards should be evaluated for effectiveness. This is another area where development of relevant metrics could yield better insights into the value of the programme for Korea's citizens. PPS, with relevant stakeholders, should study potential means of evaluating the benefits derived not just from the certification programmes, but from the variety of programmes to support secondary policy objectives.

Green standard purchasing

To leverage its purchasing power to enhance competitiveness in both local and global markets, PPS has been encouraging suppliers to develop green technology products through the mandatory purchase of products that meet a "Minimum Green Standard". Starting in 2010, PPS has designated goods which are required to meet these standards as reflected through lifecycle costing, including energy efficiency, standby power, recycling and other environmental factors. In 2013, PPS selected 25 additional products to meet the Minimum Green Standard, bringing the total number of products to 100. Purchasing of these products has increased dramatically during the life of the programme, from less than 1% of goods purchased in 2010 to more than 13% in 2013 (see Table 4.26).

Table 4.26. **Purchase of Minimum Green Standard products**

In USD millions

	2010	2011	2012	2013	2014
Total goods purchased	12 057.5	12 614.7	14 036.2	15 714.3	15 527.4
Green purchasing	33.8	1 017.2	1 339.5	2 095.7	2 500.3
Percentage	0.3%	8.1%	9.5%	13.3%	16.1%

Source: PPS response to OECD internal questionnaire, 2014 with updates in 2015.

In 2002, OECD countries adopted the Recommendation on the Environmental Performance of Public Procurement, which advocates setting green targets in procurement and adopting measures to make sure that the targets are met. Since this time, OECD countries have increasingly included environmental objectives in procurement strategies, but a number of obstacles have been identified (see Figure 4.2).

Figure 4.2. **Obstacles to green public procurement**

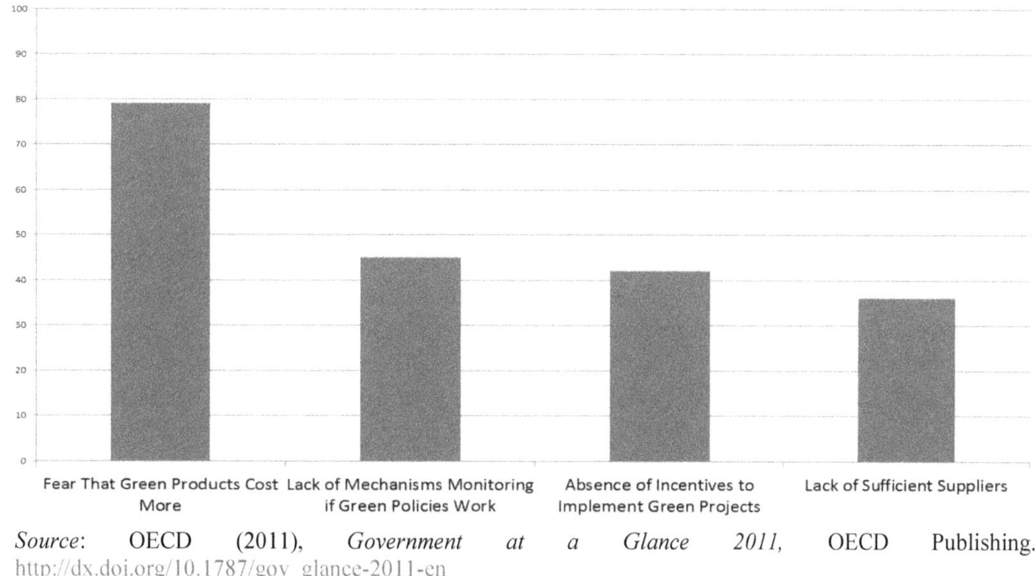

Source: OECD (2011), *Government at a Glance 2011*, OECD Publishing. http://dx.doi.org/10.1787/gov_glance-2011-en

A collection of best practices has been prepared by the OECD, providing good practices for green public procurement at national and sub-national levels. Available at www.oecd.org/gov/ethics/best-practices-for-green-procurement.htm, the practices cover the areas of:

- green public procurement legal and policy framework
- understanding market capacity and assessing costs and benefits
- introducing environmental standards in public procurement
- professionalising green public procurement
- raising awareness
- monitoring green public procurement.

Training and support

SMEs and other new entrants to public procurement have a variety of training options in Korea. PPS conducts training for suppliers, usually consisting of a two-day course covering public tenders generally and the use of the KONEPS system, at a cost of approximately USD 82.[1] The Federation of SMEs also offers training for its members in the form of a one-day, comprehensive course in how to participate in public tenders and how to use KONEPS. It is offered region by region, and each region is served by one or two courses annually. Other trade associations, such as the Construction Association of Korea, also provide training relevant for their members. Private sector training offerings on the use of KONEPS are also widely available, with third-party training providers basing their curricula on KONEPS manuals published by PPS. While interview participants generally indicated a high level of satisfaction with training opportunities, one suggested that the only concern is the rapid pace of development of new features within KONEPS, which leaves very small businesses without the resources for continuous training struggling to keep up, at times.

PPS also operates a dedicated call centre for addressing questions from public buyers and suppliers. Interview participants generally indicated a high level of satisfaction with the capabilities of the call centre staff on subjects such as the KONEPS system, how to use it, how to address system errors and the reporting of any concerns. For some legal or regulatory questions, the fact-finding mission identified a potential for improvement, as the current process of transferring the caller to the relevant division can sometimes be inefficient.

Recommendations for the improvement of training and support

PPS should consider the impact of continuous upgrades and changes to KONEPS on suppliers, particularly SMEs. While one solution would be to offer trainings more frequently for each new development, this issue could also be managed by establishing a set schedule for release of new features (perhaps semi-annually or quarterly), so SMEs and other suppliers could better anticipate the need to divert resources to learning new features.

PPS should also evaluate the process for addressing questions to the call centre that are directed to matters beyond the function of the KONEPS system. Providing expert advice on all of the specifics of public procurement, including the legal and regulatory aspects, is a very large task that will necessarily involve a referral process to identify the relevant expert, but this process could perhaps be streamlined to increase usefulness for suppliers using the system.

Potential objective overload

One concern in many OECD countries is the potential of "objective overload:" addressing so many secondary policy objectives through public procurement that the system of mandates and preferences becomes unmanageable or impossible to satisfy. There is some concern that the variety and complexity of programmes for preference in the Korean public procurement system should be carefully evaluated in light of this concern.

During the fact-finding mission, one procurement official described his need to manage the wide variety of secondary policy objectives. In an effort to support an understanding of the various requirements and to prioritise their satisfaction within the agency, this official developed a survey report to identify all of the various secondary policy requirements that applied to public procurement. This report identified 8-10 mandatory requirements, and up to 46 "recommended" procurement priorities. This report was developed independently to help him primarily to manage internal prioritisation as a procurement official at a central government agency; it does not appear that a similar listing of all applicable requirements is directly available from a central source.

One reason for this diffusion of requirements is that different ministries are tasked with different responsibilities. The Ministry of Strategy and Finance; Ministry of Industry Trade and Resources (which houses SMBA); Ministry of Culture, Sports and Tourism; and Ministry of Government Administration and Home Affairs all have control of programmes that implement preferences through public procurement. While there are meetings of the relevant stakeholders as procurement preferences are established, more can be done to ensure visibility into the various demands on the public procurement system.

Recommendation on objectives overload

PPS should establish a central listing of all mandatory and recommended goals or requirements regarding secondary policy objectives, with a brief explanation and reference linking to the origin. If possible, this list should be developed as a guide or a manual, in an interactive and informative way and also published online to achieve maximum dissemination. Furthermore, this consolidated view should be included in the training programmes as a way of improving the capacity of procurement officials to use public procurement strategically. Finally, once established, this list should be evaluated for potential opportunities to consolidate or streamline overlapping programmes, and to inform any future efforts to support additional secondary policy objectives.

Key findings and recommendations

While support for secondary policy objectives takes many forms in public procurement in Korea, this support is generally implemented in line with Element V of the OECD Recommendation, demonstrating recognition that "use of the public procurement system to pursue secondary policy objectives should be balanced against the primary procurement objective."

The adoption of new methods or goals for supporting secondary policy objectives is conducted according to a consultation process among relevant stakeholders, consistent with Element V (i), "evaluate the use of public procurement as one method of pursuing secondary policy objectives in accordance with clear national priorities." This element is also furthered by the recognition that public procurement is only one means of supporting secondary policy goals. The existence of additional programmes that are outside of the public procurement process, such as loan guarantees, indicate a balanced approach to the direct use of public procurement.

Stakeholder consultation among ministries also supports Element V (ii), "develop an appropriate strategy for the integration of secondary policy objectives in public procurement systems." This element is also supported by the mutually reinforcing nature of some programmes to support secondary policy objectives. The creation of certification programmes for small and medium-sized businesses that continue to produce innovative products is a good practice in combining support for two secondary policy objectives. Here, additional work could be done to ensure that buying entities are supported in the implementation of secondary policy objectives, for instance through the development of a central listing of all mandatory and recommended secondary policy objective goals to facilitate prioritisation.

Element V (iii) requires "appropriate impact assessment methodology to measure the effectiveness of procurement in achieving secondary policy objectives." Unlike in many OECD countries, data about the use of procurement to support secondary policy objectives is available, in the form of annual reports regarding small and medium-sized business goals, data about green public procurement, and data regarding the use of procurement to support innovation. This data is currently used to determine whether secondary policy goals are met, but a next step could involve the development of more detailed indicators, for instance to measure the cost and burden of certification procedures against the benefits they offer to small and medium-sized businesses. This element also indicates that "the aggregate effect of pursuing secondary policy objectives on the public procurement system should be periodically assessed to address potential objective overload." Given the variety and complexity of support for secondary policy objectives, such an assessment is worth pursuing, particularly with respect to the current structure of certificates and the preferences that result.

Programmes to support secondary policy objectives in Korea, in particular those that support small and medium-sized businesses, also implement Element IV of the OECD Recommendation, "facilitate access to procurement opportunities for potential competitors of all sizes." Though the variety of programmes is complex, they are generally supported by "coherent and stable institutional, legal and regulatory frameworks," consistent with IV (i). The work done by PPS to centralise and standardise procurement processes for small and medium-sized businesses also serves to implement Element IV (ii) by delivering "clear and integrated tender documentation, standardised where possible and proportionate to the need." Finally, while many of the programmes support secondary policy objectives through explicit support of particular categories of suppliers (small and medium-sized businesses, local businesses, female-owned businesses), most still involve an element of competition within the supported group, consistent with Element IV (iii). In cases where this is not true, for example in the case of direct awards to holders of the Excellent Government Product Certification, the effect of such limitations on competition should be evaluated as part of the assessment of the effectiveness of such programmes.

Summary of recommendations for action

- Consider evaluating tenders from large suppliers on the basis of support for SMEs provided through subcontracting opportunities.
- Evaluate the current structure of certificates and the preferences that result. This evaluation should include means of simplifying the certification structure, as well as means of better promoting value through a meaningful comparison of new innovations.
- Develop metrics to evaluate the effectiveness of programmes to support secondary policy objectives:
  - compare cost and burden of certification procedure against benefit
  - evaluate effectiveness of a certification procedure that leads to limited competition.
- Consider methods of mitigating the impact of continuous upgrades and changes to KONEPS on suppliers, particularly SMEs.
- Evaluate the process for addressing questions to the call centre that are directed to matters beyond the function of the KONEPS system.
- Establish a central listing of all mandatory and recommended goals or requirements regarding secondary policy objectives, in an interactive manual for procurement officials. Once established, this list should be evaluated for potential opportunities to consolidate or streamline overlapping programmes, and to inform any future efforts to support additional secondary policy objectives.

Notes

1. This figure was originally reported in USD.

References

OECD (2015a), "Recommendation of the Council on Public Procurement", www.oecd.org/corruption/recommendation-on-public-procurement.htm.

OECD (2015b), *Government at a Glance 2015*, OECD Publishing, Paris, http://dx.doi.org/10.1787/gov_glance-2015-en.

OECD (2011), *Government at a Glance 2011,* OECD Publishing. http://dx.doi.org/10.1787/gov_glance-2011-en

OECD (2015a), "Recommendation of the Council on Public Procurement", www.oecd.org/corruption/recommendation-on-public-procurement.htm.

OECD (2015b), *Government at a Glance 2015*, OECD Publishing, Paris, http://dx.doi.org/10.1787/gov_glance-2015-en.

United States Federal Acquisition Regulation 48 CFR 19.7, www.acquisition.gov/sites/default/files/current/far/html/Subpart%2019_7.html#wp1088741 (accessed 16 October 2015).

ANNEX A

MAS contracted goods and services

Product classification no. (6 digits)	Goods and services (in Korean)	Goods and services (in English)
101215	가축사료	Livestock feed
101615	교목및관목	Trees and shrubs
101616	꽃나무	Floral plants
101618	무화식물류	Non-floral plants
101715	유기질비료및식물영양제	Organic fertilizers and plant nutrients
101799	토양개량제	Soil conditioners
101917	해충및소형동물관리용품	Pest control devices
111015	광물	Minerals
111116	석재	Stone
121619	계면활성제	Surfactants
121640	살균제	Bactericides
131110	수지	Resins
141115	인쇄용지및필기용지	Printing and writing paper
141116	혁신용지	Novelty paper
141117	일반종이제품	General paper products
141118	업무용지	Business use papers
141218	코팅지	Coated papers
141219	신문용지및오프셋용지	Newsprint and offset papers
151218	방부식제	Anti-corrosives
211015	토지관리농기계	Agricultural machinery for soil preparation
211016	재배및파종기	Agricultural machinery for planting and seeding
211017	수확용농업기계	Agricultural machinery for harvesting
211018	농업용분사및분무장치	Dispersing and spraying appliances for agriculture
211022	임업용기계및장비	Forestry machinery and equipment
211023	온실장비	Greenhouse equipment
231815	음식물준비기기	Food preparation machinery
231816	음식물절단기기	Food cutting machinery
232111	전자제조및프로세싱기계	Electronic manufacturing and processing machinery
232615	쾌속조형기	Rapid prototyping machinery
241015	산업용트럭	Industrial trucks
241016	리프트장비및액세서리	Lifting equipment and accessories
241020	선반및저장장비	Shelving and storage
241115	자루	Bags
241118	탱크및원통형저장소	Tank and cylinder-type storage
241124	저장용기,캐비닛및트렁크	Storage chests, cabinets and trunks
241315	산업용냉장기	Industrial refrigerators
241416	제품완충용재료	Cushioning supplies
241499	포장부품	Packing accessories
251017	안전및소방차량	Safety and rescue vehicles
251018	오토바이류	Motorised cycles
251019	특수자동차및레저용자동차	Specialised and recreational vehicles
251726	차량장식부및외부덮개	Vehicle trim and exterior covering

Product classification no. (6 digits)	Goods and services (in Korean)	Goods and services (in English)
251731	위치추적및항법장치	Location and navigation systems and components
251750	이륜차용보조용품및액세서리	Auxiliary components and accessories for two-wheeled vehicle
261116	발전기류	Power generators
261117	배터리,전지및보조용품	Batteries, cells and accessories
261217	배선설비	Wiring equipment
271118	측정및설계공구	Measuring and layout tools
271120	조경용공구	Garden tools
271123	마킹공구	Marking tools
271127	전동공구	Power-generated tools
271132	공구키트	Tool kits
271316	에어기구및커넥터	Air fittings and connectors
301028	파일	Piling and piling accessory
301029	기둥	Post
301032	그레이팅	Grating
301036	목재건자재	Structural products
301099	골재	Aggregate
301115	콘크리트및모르타르	Concrete and mortars
301116	시멘트및석회	Cement and lime
301118	콘크리트보강철물	Concrete reinforcement hardware
301216	아스팔트류	Asphalts
301217	도로및철도건설자재	Road and railroad construction materials
301218	조경용재	Landscape architecture material
301299	특수바닥포장재	Special flooring materials
301315	블록	Blocks
301316	벽돌	Bricks
301317	타일및판석	Tiles and flagstones
301519	마무리재료및제품	Finishing materials and products
301520	울타리재료및제품	Fencing
301615	내벽마무리재료	Wall finishing materials
301616	천장재료	Ceiling materials
301617	바닥재	Flooring
301619	몰딩및목공제품	Moulding and millwork
301715	문	Doors
301716	창문	Windows
301799	문틀	Door frames
301815	위생도기	Sanitary ware
302017	상업및산업용조립건물	Prefabricated commercial and industrial structures
302220	운송건물	Transport structures
302316	이동식상용및산업용조립구조물	Portable prefabricated commercial and industrial structures
302317	천막및막구조물	Tents and membrane structures
311625	브래킷및브레이스	Brackets and braces
311628	기타철물류	Miscellaneous hardware
311632	고정장치	Retaining hardware
311634	금속망	Metal screening
312015	접착테이프	Adhesive tape
312016	기타접착제및밀폐제	Other adhesives and sealants
312115	페인트및전처리제	Paints and primers
312119	페인트도포구및페인트용품	Paint applicators and painting accessories
321015	회로어셈블리및라디오주파수부품	Circuit assemblies and radio frequency components
391016	각종등	Lamps
391115	옥내조명및설비	Interior lighting and fixtures
391116	옥외조명설비공사	Exterior lighting and fixtures
391117	비상용조명	Emergency lighting
391118	조명용액세서리	Lighting accessories
391120	이동식및임시용조명및액세서리	Portable and Temporary Lighting and accessories

Product classification no. (6 digits)	Goods and services (in Korean)	Goods and services (in English)
391121	광학조명	Optical lighting
391210	동력조절장비	Power conditioning equipment
391211	배전,조정장치및액세서리	Distribution, control centres and accessories
391214	커넥터및단자류	Connectors and terminals
391215	스위치,제어기및계전기	Switches, controls and relays
391317	배선관로및버스웨이	Wire raceways conduit and busways
401016	공기순환장치및액세서리	Air circulation, parts and accessories
401017	냉방장치	Cooling
401018	난방기구및액세서리	Heating equipment, parts and accessories
401019	습도조절장치	Humidity control
401020	보일러	Boilers
401416	밸브	Valves
401417	배관금속부품및설비	Hardware and fittings
401421	관류	Pipe
401422	유체및가스조절기	Fluid and gas regulators
401423	관이음자재	Pipe fittings
401725	관연결자재	Pipe connectors
411032	실험용세척및청소장비	Laboratory washing and cleaning equipment
411034	실험실용환경조절장치	Laboratory environmental conditioning equipment
411035	실험용환기장치및액세서리	Laboratory enclosures and accessories
411116	길이,두께및거리측정용기기	Length, thickness and distance measuring instruments
411117	망원경및현미경류	Viewing and observing instruments and accessories
411119	지시및기록용기기	Indicating and recording instruments
411121	변환기	Transducers
411125	유체측정용기기	Liquid and gas flow measuring and observing instruments
421415	애플리케이터용면봉및탈지면	Applicator swabs and cotton balls
421721	응급의료용심폐소생제품	Emergency medical services resuscitation products
421816	혈압기기및관련제품	Blood pressure units and related products
421817	심전도기및관련제품	Electrocardiography EKG units and related products
421827	검진용크기측정장치	Size-measuring devices for medical exams
421922	환자수송용품	Patient transport products
422417	하지용비내구성정형외과자재	Orthopedic softgoods for lower extremity
422418	비내구성상지및상반신용정형자재	Orthopedic softgoods for upper extremity and torso
431915	개인통신장치	Personal communication devices
431916	개인통신장치액세서리또는부품	Personal communications device accessories or parts
432018	매체저장장치	Media storage devices
432020	이동식저장매체	Removable storage media
432021	이동식저장매체액세서리	Removable storage media accessories
432115	컴퓨터	Computers
432116	컴퓨터액세서리	Computer accessories
432117	컴퓨터데이터입력장비	Computer data input devices
432118	컴퓨터데이터입력장치액세서리	Computer data input device accessories
432119	컴퓨터디스플레이	Computer displays
432120	컴퓨터디스플레이액세서리	Computer display accessories
432121	컴퓨터프린터	Computer printers
432215	콜매지니먼트시스템또는액세서리	Call management systems or accessories
432217	고정네트워크장비및부품	Fixed network equipment and components
432225	네트워크보안장비	Network security equipment
432226	네트워크서비스장비	Network service equipment
432233	데이터통신및네트워크접속장치및장비	Datacom and network connectivity installation devices and equipment
432325	교육또는조회소프트웨어	Educational or reference software
432332	보안및보호소프트웨어	Security and protection software
441015	등사기	Duplicating machines
441016	종이처리기및액세서리	Paper processing machines and accessories
441017	프린터,복사기및팩시밀리용액세서리	Printer, photocopier and facsimile accessories

Product classification no. (6 digits)	Goods and services (in Korean)	Goods and services (in English)
441018	계산기계및액세서리	Calculating machines and accessories
441020	래미네이팅용품	Laminating supplies
441021	우편기계	Mail machines
441024	라벨링기계	Labelling machines
441028	바인딩기계및라미네이션기계	Binding and lamination machines
441029	사무기기용액세서리	accessories for office equipment
441031	인쇄기,팩스및복사기 공급용품	Printer, facsimile and photocopier supplies
441032	사무용시간기록기및액세서리	Office time recording machines and accessories
441115	수납정리용품및액세서리	Organisers and accessories
441118	제도용품	Drafting supplies
441119	칠판	Boards
441215	우편용품	Mailing supplies
441216	책상용품	Desk supplies
441217	필기도구	Writing instruments
441218	수정용품	Correction supplies
441219	리필잉크및리필심	Ink and lead refills
441220	폴더바인더및인덱스	Folders, binders and indexes
441221	고정용품	Fastening supplies
451015	인쇄기계및장비	Printing machinery and equipment
451018	제본,재봉장비및보조용품	Book binding, sewing equipment and accessories
451115	낭독대음향장치및액세서리	sound systems and accessories
451116	영사기및소모품	Projectors and supplies
451117	오디오프리젠테이션및 창작장비하드웨어및컨트롤러	Audio presentation and composing equipment hardware and controllers
451118	복합영상장비및콘트롤러	Video equipment and controllers
451215	카메라	Cameras
451216	카메라액세서리	Camera accessories
451315	스틸사진용필름	Still picture film
451316	동화상용매체	Moving picture media
461517	수사장비용품및보조용품	Forensic equipment, supplies and accessories
461615	교통통제장비	Traffic control
461715	자물쇠및보안장비	Locks, security hardware and accessories
461716	감시및탐지장비	Surveillance and detection equipment
461815	보호용의류	Safety apparel
461817	두부보호장비	Face and head protection
461819	청각보호장비	Hearing protectors
461820	호흡보호장비	Respiratory protection
461822	인체공학적보조장비	Ergonomic support aids
461824	정화기기및안전청결장비	Decontamination aids and safety cleaning equipment
461825	개인보호장비또는무기	Personal safety devices or weapons
461915	화재예방장비	Fire prevention
461916	화재진압장비	Fire-fighting equipment
471015	수처리및공급장비	Water treatment and supply equipment
471016	용수처리용품	Water treatment consumables
471216	마루청소용기계및액세서리	Floor cleaning machines and accessories
471217	쓰레기용기및액세서리	Waste containers and accessories
471315	청소용걸레,천및닦개	Cleaning rags, cloths and wipes
471316	비대걸레솔및액세서리	Brooms, mops, brushes and accessories
471317	화장실용품	Restroom supplies
471318	세척제및소독제	Cleaning and disinfecting solutions
481015	상업용조리기기	Cooking equipment
481016	상업용식료품가공기기	Food processing equipment
481017	상업용식음료품조제기기	Food and beverage dispensing equipment
481018	상업용취사도구및주방기구	Cookware and kitchen tools
481020	식당용가구	Restaurant furniture

Product classification no. (6 digits)	Goods and services (in Korean)	Goods and services (in English)
481021	저장,취급장비및용품	Storage, handling equipment and supplies
489998	묘지용품	Products for grave
491215	캠핑용품	Camping products
491416	윈드서핑및기타수중스포츠장비	Windsurfing and other water sports equipment
491615	필드운동장비	Field sports equipment
491616	라켓및코트운동장비	Racquet and court sports equipment
491715	체조장비	Gymnastics equipment
491815	테이블게임용구	Equipment for table games
492015	유산소운동기구	Aerobic training equipment
492016	근력강화용헬스기구	Weight lifting equipment
492215	스포츠액세서리	Sports accessories
492415	운동장및놀이터용장비	Playground equipment
502017	커피및차	Coffee and tea
512805	기타대사성의약품	Other metabolic medicine
513103	생물학적제제류	Biological medicine
513104	항기생동물성약품류	Parasite medicine
513202	진단용액	Diagnostic drugs
513203	공중위생용약	Public sanitary cares
521215	침구류	Bedclothes
521216	식탁보,주방용천및액세서리	Table, kitchen linen and accessories
521315	커튼및긴커튼	Curtains and draperies
521316	블라인드및차양	Blinds and shades
521317	창문관련소품	Window supplies
521416	가정용세탁기기및용품	Domestic laundry appliances and supplies
521418	기타분류안된가전기기	Other domestic household appliances
521518	가정용취사도구	Domestic cookware
521520	가정용식기류	Domestic bakeware
521522	설거지및식기수납보조용품	Dishwashing and dish storage accessories
521615	음향기기및영상기기	Audio and visual equipment
521616	영상음향장비용액세서리	Audio visual equipment accessories
531015	슬랙스,바지및반바지	Slacks, trousers and shorts
531018	코트및재킷	Coats and jackets
531023	속옷	Undergarments
531024	양말류	Hosiery
531025	의류액세서리	Clothing accessories
531027	유니폼	Uniforms
531029	운동복	Athletic wear
531031	조끼	Waistcoats
531116	구두	Shoes
531117	슬리퍼	Slippers
531119	운동화	Athletic footwear
531215	여행가방	Luggage
531217	사무용가방	Business cases
531218	여행용품세트및여행용품세트부속품	Travel kits and accessories
531315	구강및치과위생용제품	Dental products
531316	목욕및바디용품	Bath and body products
531415	재봉파스너	Sewing fasteners
541015	순보석	Fine jewellery
541115	휴대용시계	Watches
551015	인쇄출판물	Printed publications
551215	꼬리표	Tags
551216	라벨	Labels
551217	신호표지	Signage
551218	신분증명문서	Identification documents
551219	표식장비	Signage equipment

Product classification no. (6 digits)	Goods and services (in Korean)	Goods and services (in English)
561015	가구	Furniture
561016	옥외용가구	Outdoor furniture
561017	사무용가구	Office furniture
561116	패널시스템	Panel Systems
561121	좌석	Seating
561210	도서관가구	Library furnishings
561214	카페테리아및간이식당설비	Cafeteria and lunchroom furnishings
561215	교실용가구	General classroom furnishings
561216	보육원용놀이및취침설비	Creative play and rest time furnishings for daycare and early childhood facilities
561217	교실용서적및기타물품보관장비	Book and general storage units for classrooms
561218	직업교육시설및설비	Vocational classroom furnishings and fixtures
561220	연구실용가구	Laboratory furniture
601016	교육인증서또는학위증서	Educational certificates or diplomas
601017	교사용지침교재	Resource materials for teachers
601024	기초수학,계산지침교재및부교재	Early learning math, calculation resources and auxiliary textbooks
601027	도형,조화,공간인식또는논리적사고를 위한교사지침서	Pattern, matching or spatial perception or logical thinking resource materials for teachers
601037	외국어에관한교재	Foreign languages resources
601041	신체조직및관련자료	Body systems and related materials
601044	지질학및지구과학	Geology and earth science
601061	직업교육자료	Vocational teaching aids and materials
601093	멀티미디어학습시스템및용품	Multimedia education systems and supplies
601098	학습교구	Instruction materials for education
601211	캔버스,필름,보드및아트지	Canvases, films, boards and art papers
601212	수업용,세공용페인트,용구및보조품	Supplies and applicators for classroom and fine art paint
601214	사진틀	Picture frames
601215	그림도구,용품및보조품	Drawing tools, supplies and accessories
601222	나무공예	Wood crafts
601243	점토,성형콤파운드,세라믹장비및보조품	Clay, modeling compounds, ceramics equipment and accessories
601310	건반악기	Keyboard instruments
601314	타악기	Percussion instruments
601411	게임	Games
721029	부지관리관련용역	Facility maintenance and repair services
721512	냉난방.환풍.공기조절시스템설치용역	Heating, cooling and air conditioning HVAC installation services
731615	기계제조	Manufacture of machinery
761115	일반건물및사무실청소업	General building and office cleaning and maintenance services
781018	도로화물수송	Road cargo transport
801715	여론분석및홍보계획서비스	Opinion analysis and promotion planning services
811120	데이터서비스	Data service
821118	편집및지원서비스	Editorial and support services
841316	생명,건강및사고보험	Life, health and accident insurance
861016	과학분야직업훈련업	Scientific vocational training services
861115	원거리학습서비스	Distance learning services
861417	교육공학	Educational technology
901115	숙박업	Hotels, motels, and inns

ORGANISATION FOR ECONOMIC CO-OPERATION AND DEVELOPMENT

The OECD is a unique forum where governments work together to address the economic, social and environmental challenges of globalisation. The OECD is also at the forefront of efforts to understand and to help governments respond to new developments and concerns, such as corporate governance, the information economy and the challenges of an ageing population. The Organisation provides a setting where governments can compare policy experiences, seek answers to common problems, identify good practice and work to co-ordinate domestic and international policies.

The OECD member countries are: Australia, Austria, Belgium, Canada, Chile, the Czech Republic, Denmark, Estonia, Finland, France, Germany, Greece, Hungary, Iceland, Ireland, Israel, Italy, Japan, Korea, Luxembourg, Mexico, the Netherlands, New Zealand, Norway, Poland, Portugal, the Slovak Republic, Slovenia, Spain, Sweden, Switzerland, Turkey, the United Kingdom and the United States. The European Union takes part in the work of the OECD.

OECD Publishing disseminates widely the results of the Organisation's statistics gathering and research on economic, social and environmental issues, as well as the conventions, guidelines and standards agreed by its members.

OECD PUBLISHING, 2, rue André-Pascal, 75775 PARIS CEDEX 16
(42 2015 25 1 P) ISBN 978-92-64-24941-7 – 2016

www.ingramcontent.com/pod-product-compliance
Lightning Source LLC
LaVergne TN
LVHW081411110826
845149LV00010B/1702
* 9 7 8 9 2 6 4 2 4 9 4 1 7 *